Virtue and Vice in Popular Film

This book addresses a prominent group of virtues and vices as portrayed in popular films to further our understanding of these moral character traits. The discussions emphasize the interplay between the philosophical conception of the virtues and vices and the cinematic representations of character.

Joseph H. Kupfer explores how fictional characters possessing certain moral strengths and weaknesses concretize our abstract understanding of them. Because the actions that flow from these traits occur in cinematic contexts mirroring real world conditions, the narrative portrayals of these moral characteristics can further our appreciation of their import. Humility, integrity, and perseverance, for example, are depicted in *Chariots of Fire, The Fabulous Baker Boys*, and *Billy Elliot*, while the vices of envy, arrogance, and vanity are captured in *Amadeus, Whiplash,* and *Young Adult*.

This interdisciplinary work in philosophy and film criticism will be of great interest to scholars and students of film studies, philosophy of film, ethics, aesthetics, and popular culture.

Joseph H. Kupfer is University Professor of Philosophy at Iowa State University. He has previously written on such topics as privacy, lying, the parent-child relationship, aesthetics of nature, and the virtues. His most recent book, *Aesthetic Violence and Women in Film: Kill Bill with Flying Daggers,* addresses philosophical issues in popular action movies.

Routledge Focus on Film Studies

1 **Robot Ecology and the Science Fiction Film**
   J. P. Telotte

2 **Weimar Cinema, Embodiment, and Historicity**
   Cultural Memory and the Historical Films of Ernst Lubitsch
   Mason Kamana Allred

3 **Migrants in Contemporary Spanish Film**
   Clara Guillén Marín

4 **Virtue and Vice in Popular Film**
   Joseph H. Kupfer

Virtue and Vice in Popular Film

Joseph H. Kupfer

LONDON AND NEW YORK

First published 2021
by Routledge
2 Park Square, Milton Park, Abingdon, Oxon OX14 4RN

and by Routledge
605 Third Avenue, New York, NY 10158

Routledge is an imprint of the Taylor & Francis Group, an informa business

© 2021 Joseph H. Kupfer

The right of Joseph H. Kupfer to be identified as author of this work has been asserted by him in accordance with sections 77 and 78 of the Copyright, Designs and Patents Act 1988.

All rights reserved. No part of this book may be reprinted or reproduced or utilised in any form or by any electronic, mechanical, or other means, now known or hereafter invented, including photocopying and recording, or in any information storage or retrieval system, without permission in writing from the publishers.

Trademark notice: Product or corporate names may be trademarks or registered trademarks, and are used only for identification and explanation without intent to infringe.

British Library Cataloguing-in-Publication Data
A catalogue record for this book is available from the British Library

Library of Congress Cataloging-in-Publication Data
A catalog record has been requested for this book

ISBN: 9780367543709 (hbk)
ISBN: 9780367543730 (pbk)
ISBN: 9781003088998 (ebk)

Typeset in Times New Roman
by codeMantra

For Judy

Contents

	Introduction	1
1	Taking humility in stride in *Chariots of Fire*	9
2	Arrogance in the classroom: *The Prime of Miss Jean Brodie* and *Whiplash*	24
3	Art and integrity in *The Fabulous Baker Boys*	44
4	*Amadeus* as a portrait of envy	63
5	The virtues of aspiration: three boys make good	80
6	The calamity of vanity in *Young Adult*	102
	Index	117

Introduction

Philosophy and film

In discussing virtue and vice in mass marketed films, this book attempts to accomplish two, entwined, purposes: to develop our understanding of these moral traits by examining movies and to enrich our experience of movies by employing moral theory to interpret them. The book, then, offers a philosophical exploration of moral psychology in concert with doing film criticism. The benefits of the book for virtue ethics and film study are the result of the interplay between film criticism and philosophical theorizing about moral character.

I have chosen films whose portrayals of virtue and vice seem to me to accurately reflect the way these moral dispositions operate in the real world. Interpreting the fictional worlds of these films, I believe, broadens our understanding of virtue and vice, revealing connections among them that might otherwise go unnoticed. When we see how Salieri is riven with envy for Mozart, for example, we realize how the threat to one's self-image can drive a person to justify his resentment. At the same time, the representation of Salieri vivifies the way in which envy can comport with unabashed admiration. The vanity of Mavis and her subsequent public exposure reveal how vanity and shame mirror one another: where vanity craves the gaze of other people, shame shrinks from it, seeking concealment. The provisional view of the virtues and vices I bring to the films, therefore, is subject to modification and amplification through the cinematic interpretations.

Bringing virtue theory to bear on film criticism also adds to our appreciation of the films. Articulating the visions of virtue and vice embodied in the movie stories provides a fresh angle on the films. The ideas about moral psychology that are disclosed in the philosophical analyses of the films enlarge our aesthetic appreciation because they make significant contributions to cinematic aspects of the movies. The philosophical perspective on the virtues and vices that I attribute to the film affords a framework for integrating dimensions of character, plot, dialogue, and cinematic structure. The interpretations of film that are offered in the following chapters involve presenting philosophical concepts and themes, and showing how they relate to the cinematically rendered aspects of the film fiction. Because virtue theory is the foundation of the interpretations of film presented in this book, I will now offer a brief sketch of the nature of virtue and vice as well as the distinctive cast of the particular traits examined in the films.

Virtue and vice

Virtues are excellent traits of character that are good for the individuals who possess them, for other people, or both. They are relatively stable dispositions of habits to think, feel, desire, and act in ways that form discernible patterns. Some moral virtues supply the individual with purposes or attitudes that motivate action in particular directions. These substantive virtues include generosity, loyalty, and humility. For example, the virtue of generosity prompts people to give what is valuable to others, in order to help or please them. Loyalty moves us to think the best of our friends and to support them when things are not going well for them. Humility involves keeping our own strengths and weaknesses in proper perspective. When we do especially well, for example, humility curbs our desire to advertise it or to denigrate those whose ability or performance is less than our own. The first chapter, dealing with *Chariots of Fire*, explores how even people with exceptional talent and accomplishment can remain humble.

In contrast to such substantive virtues that contain purposes or specific content are executive virtues. These moral dispositions enable us to perform actions and pursue ends whatever they may be. They are instrumental in carrying out our plans and because doing so may be difficult, they are also considered virtues of willpower. Virtues such as perseverance, patience, and resourcefulness enable us to surmount obstacles and continue to work toward the realization of our goals or projects. In Chapter Five, we see how these very virtues are essential to the success enjoyed by the boys who aspire to master rocketry, dance, and chess in their respective film-stories. Without these virtues, the boys would not have the willpower or fortitude needed to develop the abilities that are ingredient to their flourishing in their various disciplines. Here we should also distinguish moral virtues from non-moral virtues. Intellectual virtues are requisite for science, mathematics, or chess. Aesthetic virtues are responsible for people excelling in creating or appreciating the arts, such as dance, or beauty in general.

Moral virtues obviously benefit the people who have them. Because executive virtues such as patience and resourcefulness enable us to achieve our ends, they obviously contribute to our overall well-being. Few long-range projects are achievable without an array of these virtues. Some executive virtues are social in nature, such as cooperativeness, necessarily promoting the good of those who possess the virtue as well as the individuals with whom they interact. Substantive virtues, such as generosity and justice, clearly make life better for the people who are at the receiving end of our generous and just actions. But even as these virtues are benefitting others, they are indirectly enhancing our own lives. Because we are generous, just, or loyal, we receive the gratitude and affection of those who have more directly enjoyed the results of our virtuous actions. Consequently, it is hard to imagine a good life that is deficient in, let alone devoid of, a significant number of both executive and substantive virtues.

It follows, then, that vices are the debilitating corollaries of virtues. They are entrenched dispositions that are harmful to those who possess them, other individuals, or both. Vices that correspond to executive virtues make us unlikely to achieve goals that require sustained effort over long stretches of time. For example, vices such as impatience undermine the capacity to persist in demanding labors when more attractive, more available but fleeting gratifications present themselves. Surliness and uncooperativeness keep people from the harmonious social interaction that is often needed to realize one's own ends and those of other people. Most blatantly among substantive vices, stinginess and callousness keep us from helping other people and this, in turn, has a negative impact on how other people view us and our own interests.

The virtues and vices considered in this book have a distinctive direction – they are self-regarding, primarily about the self and the relationship we have with ourselves. Of course, they have implications for thought, feeling, and behavior that affect other people, but the focus of their operation and regard is the self who possesses them. Many virtues direct attention and action outwardly, toward other people or circumstances. Justice, for example, concerns the distribution of benefits and burdens at large in one's community or in a broader context. The virtues of care and generosity orient us toward the suffering or needs of other individuals and move us to try to be of help. So, too, does cooperativeness dispose us to get along with other people and work with them in productive ways. But concern with the self characterizes the virtues and vices discussed in this book.

The structure of the book

Here are the virtues and vices that are examined through the films I have chosen. Humility and its corresponding vice of arrogance are constituted by the perspective we have on our own worth, whether moral or technical (having to do with some domain of competence or expertise involving a particular set of skills). Humility reflects an accurate view of our technical abilities as well as our moral character. The humble individual has a realistic assessment of her strengths and limits, prizing her abilities and virtues, but accepting their limitations in a down-to-earth manner. She is also disposed to give credit to others for their help and to be grateful for her natural gifts. In the film *Chariots of Fire*, discussed in Chapter One, Eric Liddell is portrayed as a paragon of humility. Although he is an outstanding runner, he does not let success go to his head because he keeps his accomplishments in proper perspective. Liddell is thankful for his natural gifts, but recognizes that there are more important things in life and the world than being fleet of foot. His demeanor and behavior express his humility; he treats others with respect even when he thinks they are morally wrong and he subordinates his personal aspirations to transcendent moral and religious ideals.

Where humility has a realistic view of our moral and non-moral worth, arrogance inflates our moral standing due to an exaggerated sense of our non-moral abilities. Because the arrogant individual thinks too highly of himself, he sees himself as morally superior to others; as a result, he is imperious with and demanding of other people. Such a person "arrogates" to himself privilege and command to which he is not truly entitled. Arrogance is especially worrisome in teachers, the main characters in the films examined in Chapter Two. Jean Brodie and Terence Fletcher, in *The Prime of Miss Jean Brodie* and *Whiplash*, respectively, impose their will and beliefs on their students instead of encouraging their young pupils to figure things out for themselves. They seem to value their celebrated status in their respective schools more for their own self-aggrandizement than as the opportunity to nurture their students' intellectual and aesthetic abilities. The pair of authoritarian pedants not only shortchanges their students pedagogically, but endangers them because of their arrogance. Arrogance and its antithesis, humility, will figure significantly in subsequent chapters, as auxiliary to the main vices and virtues under discussion.

Integrity characterizes an individual whose major commitments, moral and otherwise, are consistent with one another and honored in his actions. We act with integrity when we are "true to" ourselves: our moral principles as well as our deepest passions. Integrity is an exception among the virtues. By itself, it does not seem to be either a substantive or executive virtue. Integrity does not provide purposeful motivation, nor is it instrumental in enabling us to realize our goals. It does, however, depend upon the substantive virtues in addition to the non-moral commitments the individual has. In this sense, then, integrity supervenes upon specific virtues or abilities that make up the core of our person. Integrity or its lack, therefore, in a sense "sums up" who we are, defining us as intact or at odds with ourselves. The arc of the story of *The Fabulous Baker Boys*, the subject of Chapter Three, traces the recovery of Jack Baker's integrity. For too long, he has denied his talent and passion for creatively playing jazz rather than the popular fare he dishes out nightly with his less gifted brother. Because his actions and feelings are at odds with this central dimension of who Jack is, he is often surly and aloof. By film's end, however, he is finally true to himself, breaking with the Baker boys' dual piano act to strike out on his own, more inventive, musical path.

At first blush, envy would appear to be about other people rather than ourselves. After all, when we envy someone we want what they have, feel animosity, or resentment toward them, and wish them harm or at least to be deprived of the cherished thing. Although envy takes another person and his possession of something we covet as its immediate object, the soil from which it springs is our regard for ourselves. It is about self-regard in that we lack the desirable thing and are preoccupied with our deprivation and the fact that someone else enjoys what we wish we had. Consequently, we feel aggrieved over not having the object of our envy, believing ourselves somehow entitled to it. Therefore, envy cannot arise without a particular configuration of desires and attitudes at the center of which is how we view ourselves. Chapter Four takes the character of Salieri in *Amadeus* as offering a complex and illuminating portrait of envy. It is made especially poignant by virtue of the fact that

Salieri adores Mozart's music as much as he despises its amazing creator. Because Mozart makes Salieri see himself as less than the outstanding composer he had been heralded as, Salieri undermines the prodigy's career and hastens his demise, ironically, by helping him complete a musical masterpiece.

The executive virtue of perseverance is central in the three films of Chapter Five, in which a trio of boys pursue excellence in their respective fields. Inspired by rocketry, dance, and chess, the boys embark on careers that demand tenacity and willpower in *October Skies, Billy Elliot,* and *Searching for Bobby Fischer,* respectively. Perseverance is the ability to soldier on with challenging work when it does not go well, when it would be easy to give up. Two of the three boys must overcome poverty and skeptical fathers, and all three have to deal with the self-doubt and discouragement that arise from the inevitable setbacks or missteps that occur in their vocational pursuits. The films show that perseverance rests upon a base of three auxiliary virtues: humility, patience, and resilience. Humility has already been noted. Patience concerns time: the ability to wait calmly for events to unfold or to take the time necessary to do the things needed for success. Resilience is the capacity to rebound from misadventure or outright failure. When resilient, we acknowledge how we have come up short, but are able to return to our undertaking with renewed resolve and energy. Homer, Billy, and Josh exhibit patience with themselves, the time it takes to master a discipline. They all succeed because they have the humility to accept help and the resilience to recover from temporary defeats.

Vanity is another virtue that focuses on the self. The vain individual takes too much pride and delight in a desirable attribute or thing that she possesses: appearance, accomplishment, or accumulation of something that the world esteems. And yet, vanity demands an audience; the individual seeks to be recognized and admired for the object of vanity. The vain person cares too much about her possession and stakes too much of her personal worth on it. In two respects, vanity is the opposite of envy. First, vanity preens over something the individual values and actually does possess, instead of yearning for what is lacking (as in envy). Second, the vain person wants to be seen and admired; the vice therefore radiates outward from the overblown self-regard. In contrast, envy's outward gaze upon the other person who enjoys what we prize, turns us back upon ourselves, making us feel inferior because we do not have the cherished object. The vanity of Mavis Gary in *Young Adult* is shown to prompt her to behavior that is self-destructive and callous toward others in Chapter Six. Repeatedly primping and buffing her attractive appearance, her attempts to rekindle an old romance expose her as the deluded and self-centered person she is. Although she has a striking moment of clarity about herself, it is soon occluded by the pull and familiarity of her vain preoccupation.

Film and virtue: narrative affinity

There are various aspects to moral living and the ethical theories that seek to account for it. Moral matters include actions, consequences, rules, laws, rights, duties, justifications, and excuses. The examination of virtue and vice, however, is uniquely situated to benefit from the concrete contexts afforded by narrative. This is because stories provide a parallel to real life biographies and understanding the moral character of actual people requires situating it within some form of personal history. Ascribing virtues and vices to people we know or learn about presupposes constructing stories for them. We cannot know whether someone is courageous or patient simply by looking at a thin time slice of their behavior. Rather, we need to see how they act over an extended period, in a variety of circumstances: how they interact with a diverse cast of people.

For example, standing up to danger could well be an idiosyncratic, isolated occurrence for a particular individual. Her more typically craven, chronic behavior would change our opinion of her were it available to us. The same thing goes for patience. Knowing that an acquaintance is usually able to bear delays with equanimity in having his desires met enables us to discount his rare display of pique when something important to him is unnecessarily forestalled. The wider and deeper context constitutive of a more or less robust narrative is vital to a proper perspective on someone's moral character.

Because of our reliance on narrative to make sense of the moral traits of actual people, examining stories such as found in film fictions is most fitting in analyzing virtue and vice. Along with written and spoken narrative, cinematic tales provide something like an imaginative laboratory for dissecting moral character. Instead of the necessarily abbreviated examples found in most philosophical accounts of the virtues and vices, movie stories afford extended, indepth illustrations of these important dispositions. In offering finegrained, complex quasi-biographies, cinematic stories complement typically more abstract philosophical accounts of moral psychology. Film presents artistically shaped representations of human life, filled with the subtlety, ambiguity, and complications that so often define everyday experience. By doing so, narrative is able to amplify and elaborate upon our understanding of virtue and vice. It can reveal ways in which these habits influence our behavior, interact with one another, and also differ from one another.

Ethical theory and movie experience mutually inform one another. Even as film-stories help further our understanding of virtue and vice, so the philosophical accounts of these decisive moral traits can enlarge our interpretation and appreciation of cinema. Theoretical structure has the capability of taking us more deeply into the motivations, intentions, and reactions of the fictional characters on the screen. Our theory-laden understanding of arrogance, for instance, gives us a fuller appreciation of how and why Brodie and Fletcher go wrong, despite their obvious pedagogical gifts. A philosophical view of integrity, for another example, makes sense of Jack Baker's detached attitude and persistent malaise.

The main characters in all the films canvassed here are engaged in important, demanding undertakings. For most of them, the work constitutes an essential pursuit, an activity that is fundamental to their lives; the character is driven, as the activity is central to his identity and flourishing. Music is the existentially basic pursuit in the chapters on integrity (Chapter Three) and envy (Chapter Four). Competitive running at the Olympic level is the focus of the first chapter, on humility, and the main characters of the second chapter, on arrogance, are teachers. The three boys featured in the chapter on aspiration (Chapter Five) are respectively devoted to science, dance, and chess. Although Mavis is not as enamored of writing the way the other characters are committed to their pursuits, creating novels for adolescent girls is, after all, her occupation and it does fuel her vanity, as investigated in the last chapter. For all of these characters, therefore, the essential pursuit helps make their lives meaningful. These long-term, rigorous endeavors are inextricably bound up with the exercise of their relevant virtues and vices. We could say that pursuing music or teaching, dance or chess, gives direction and context to the moral character traits examined in these films. For the most part, then, the disciplines that are central to these characters' lives govern the actions that cultivate or exhibit the protagonists' dominant moral traits.

1 Taking humility in stride in *Chariots of Fire*

Two great runners

As the legendary sprinter, Harold Abrahams (Ben Cross), is lauded at his memorial service, Hugh Hudson's *Chariots of Fire* (1981) fades in a flashback to the emblematic scene of Britain's Olympic hopefuls running along the sea. Accompanied by the triumphant strains of the film's swelling musical anthem, this heroic segment seems an unlikely prelude to a sustained exploration of so quiet a virtue as humility.[1] In its exploration, the film thoughtfully addresses the question of whether humility is compatible with outstanding achievement, including awareness of one's superiority.

Outshining one's competitors appears to be a force for high self-regard, but if humility entailed ignorance of one's ability or self-deception it would be suspect as a genuine virtue. In its characterization of the Scottish runner, Eric Liddell (Ian Charleson), the film illustrates how an individual can be realistic in assessing his considerable achievements and remain humble. It also shows how humility promotes other virtues and inhibits vice. By deepening our understanding of virtue, moreover, the film also demonstrates the general way in which narrative can expand philosophical reflection on moral matters.

Liddell is introduced immediately after we watch Harold Abrahams' successful challenge for the "college dash" – completing a sprint around the perimeter of the Caius courtyard at Oxford within twelve seconds. Abrahams is the first man to accomplish the feat in 700 years. The two finest British runners are thereby cinematically joined, and much can be said both ethically and aesthetically in comparing the pair. I will confine considerations of Abrahams, however, to his significance for humility and Liddell's character (rather than, say, to examine arrogance, dedication, or anti-Semitism).

In marked contrast to Abrahams's cocky challenge of the college dash, Liddell must be cajoled into running shortly after his stint of officiating at a footrace for young boys. As Liddell runs, we are introduced to what will be identifiable as his musical motif: a sweet slow trumpet, joined by a welling passage on electronic keyboard. Liddell's arms flail and his mouth opens – our first glimpse of his ungainly yet captivating style. It will come to symbolize the ecstasy Liddell experiences in running, an ecstasy that is athletic, aesthetic, and religious all at once.

Having gradually linked Liddell and Abrahams by juxtaposing episodes in which they are featured, the film brings them together in the scene in which Abrahams watches Liddell run an incredible race in a competition between Scotland and France. After being shoved to the ground in an unsportsmanlike act by a French runner, Liddell gets up, makes up the seemingly insurmountable lead, and nearly kills himself in overtaking the field. Again we hear Liddell's theme, briefly and poignantly, as Liddell's flapping arms and gaping mouth now are accompanied by his signature tilting back of his head. He faces heavenward, as if deriving his strength and willpower directly from a God above.

Abrahams seems to epitomize the reaction of the audience, of the race and the film, in his riveted attention to Liddell's valiant run. Our awe at Liddell's surpassing effort is mirrored in Abrahams's astonished gaze. The film thereby elevates the character of Liddell as the object of observation by the film's other protagonist and not solely by the audience of the film. As with the film's audience, Abrahams sees something more than an outstanding runner when he watches the flying Scotsman. Liddell's running reveals his character, and the humility of that character determines both Liddell's decision not to run on the Sabbath and how he deals with great achievement when he does compete.

The moral perspective of humility

Norvin Richards argues that humility is a virtue because its avoidance of self-inflation does not entail a false, denigrated view of oneself. The individual is able to "resist temptations to overestimate oneself and one's accomplishments" by comparing his accomplishments to those of more outstanding people (1988: 255). No matter how good my philosophical writing, it does not compare to Aristotle's, and no matter how good your golfing, it is not Arnold Palmer's.

Of course, we can then ask whether Aristotle or Palmer could know how good he really is and still be humble.

As a paradigm of humility, the various facets of Eric Liddell's nature and his interactions with other people suggest a more complex moral response to this question about humility and self-knowledge than that offered by Richards.[2] Liddell wins an Olympic medal in track and his depiction in the film is of someone whose humility is not even ruffled by the winds of success, let alone strained by them. According to Richards, Liddell can remain humble by keeping in mind the superior performances of other runners, past and contemporary. But such comparison is narrow and limited. It does not seem to fully capture how humble people keep a level head about their achievements, and the character of Liddell in the film shows us why. Let us call this the technical or achievement consideration – comparing our performance in some particular area of skill or ability to the accomplishments of other people. My suggestion is that this non-moral weighing is subordinate to a richer moral perspective and all but disappears as pertinent in light of the moral viewpoint.

The moral perspective that animates humility has two predominant dimensions: a moral standard or ideal and our fundamental dependence. We can maintain our humility by gauging ourselves by an independent, supreme ideal. For Liddell, this is God's perfection or the perfection to which He bids us aspire. Of course, we can also compare our moral character to that of other people (such as saints), but such a self-assessment is really but a step on the way to the full ideal, or a shadow cast by it. To be sure, the moral standard need not involve a divine being, as Aristotle's portrait of the virtuous individual attests. Whether religious or secular, the idea is that individuals govern their self-assessment by moral values that are objective, general, and action-guiding. Doing so, I argue, enables even people of outstanding technical or moral achievement to remain humble.

The moral viewpoint also includes acknowledging our fundamental dependence on forces that undergird our ability and success. Liddell has an abiding sense of his fundamental dependence on God for his natural ability and for the discipline needed to develop it. Liddell can sustain humility in his accomplishments because he gives appropriate credit for them to God. Secular individuals can keep in mind their dependence on the fortuitous influences in their lives, sensitive to the fact that with a twist of fate, or DNA, they would not enjoy the success they do. However much we accomplish, it depends to a great extent on our genetic endowment, parental nurture, education, and just plain luck to have the requisite opportunities to shine. Fundamental dependence is moral because it involves appreciating that we are not responsible for the aspects of life on which we depend; therefore, they are not deserved.

As I discuss Liddell, I will speak of him and his humility as he is portrayed in the film, and apparently was in life, brimming with devotion to God. But I will also speak of him as an exemplar of humility *simpliciter* because we wish to see how humility can function without religious conviction. Consequently, for all his faith and devotion, the character of Eric Liddell also discloses how a non-religious individual can keep his technical achievement in perspective by viewing it in a moral light. Examining Liddell as our moral paradigm can thereby clarify the role religious conviction is liable to play in the structure of humility without confining our understanding to religious humility.

Companion virtues

The very religious conviction that grounds Liddell's humbling moral outlook also jeopardizes his running. As luck (or Providence) would have it, the qualifying Olympic heats for Liddell's race are scheduled to be run on the Sabbath, and he refuses to break with God's prohibition. The film mines the conflict between Liddell and the British Olympic officials. Not only is Liddell genuinely sorry for not being able to run and for disappointing his countrymen, but his gentle demeanor contrasts with the unsympathetic attitude of the disgruntled officials. One of them, in fact, is simply incredulous that Liddell would let his religious beliefs stand in the way of competing for his nation's honor.

In the course of resolving Liddell's quandary, the film discloses deeper layers of his humility. At the same time, it uses the episode of Liddell's predicament to illuminate how humility encourages other virtues while inhibiting vice. The episode discloses these connections between humility and other moral traits through its depiction of a pivotal supporting character as well as Liddell. One suggestion for reconciling Liddell's religious compunctions with his chance to run involves simply asking the French officials who are hosting the Olympics to change Liddell's qualifying heat. But the British committeemen reject the humbling alternative of asking for a favor out of pride cloaked as a matter of "national dignity." The film thereby underscores Liddell's humility by contrasting it with the pigheaded pride of his countrymen.

Well, what is to be done? Just as the impasse seems unbreachable, in walks Lord Andrew Lindsay (Nigel Havers), the teammate of Harold Abrahams's whose funeral oration opens the film. Lindsay offers to give his place in a different race, to be run on a different day, to Liddell. Lindsay first excuses his generosity by pointing out that he has already bagged a silver medal. He then forestalls Liddell's protest, saying, "A pleasure... just to see you run." In an understated, almost casual manner, Lindsay's behavior points to ways in which humility promotes the virtue of generosity and curbs the vice of envy.

Respect and appreciation for what is objectively valuable for its own sake informs humility. As Thomas Hill perceptively observes, humility is "an attitude which measures the importance of things independently of their relation to oneself..." (1991: 112). Because they have the proper attitude toward themselves and their abilities, people with humility are disposed to see value in natural and human creations and events apart from themselves. Humble individuals value and support things such as natural beauty, science, art, or God – because they are objectively worthwhile, independent of themselves. Liddell appreciates what is valuable apart from himself, since it is created by God or reflects His goodness. In the scene of Lindsay's rescue of the day, we see that Lindsay also honors what is objectively valuable – Liddell's enormous talent. It seems fair to say that humility engenders gratitude through its regard for things that evoke our admiration or awe that "extend beyond the self" (Snow 1995: 206).

Liddell's humility clearly makes him grateful to God for all the manifestations of His goodness, including Liddell's own talent. Lindsay expresses gratitude for Liddell's running ability and the chance to see Liddell compete at the highest level. Lindsay's generosity flows from his gratitude for Liddell's gift. We can be generous with things other than money such as thought, emotion, and recognition; Lindsay is willing to give his opportunity to compete for the sake of something he deems special. None of this could happen unless Lindsay enjoyed an unalloyed appreciation for Liddell's talent. What makes this additionally important will emerge more explicitly and painfully when we examine the envy that Salieri feels for Mozart's musical genius (in Chapter Four, on *Amadeus*).

Lack of humility keeps Salieri from simply admiring the other composer's immense ability, the way Lindsay is able to fully and unconditionally value Liddell's running. Indirectly, and perhaps only through reflection on such people as Salieri, *Chariots of Fire* indicates how humility is a curb on envy. Because of Lindsay's humble and accurate understanding of his own running ability, he is open and free to unencumbered appreciation of someone who surpasses him in something he prizes. With such sweet appreciation does Lindsay thereby demonstrate that he is himself humbled before the athletic ability of Liddell, from which his act of generosity springs so fully and graciously.

The two small lessons about humility that are nested within Liddell's quandary artfully complement one another. For even as the pride of the British officials keeps them from humbling themselves by asking the French for a favor, so does Lord Lindsay's humble regard for Liddell's talent prompt his generosity. Lack of humility threatens to deprive the British, the world, and Liddell of the chance for him to compete. The presence of humility, encouraging generosity, restores that chance. All does finally end well, of course, as Liddell wins his race, despite the fact that it is a longer distance than he is accustomed to running – yet another obstacle for him to surmount.

The scene of Liddell's quandary over competing on the Sabbath also discloses yet another virtue that humility fosters: being non-judgmental or charitable in our estimation of others. Liddell clearly thinks that he is right to refuse to run on the Sabbath, and that his interpretation of Scripture is the correct one. Like most religious people, Liddell is no relativist. It follows then that he believes professed Christians (or Jews) who compete on the Sabbath or urge others to compete are morally wrong to disobey God. This incident raises a question that parallels the problem that we saw posed for humility by awareness of one's technical excellence. But because the stakes are now raised to the level of morality, we cannot simply recognize that our superiority is eclipsed by the moral excellence of other people or an overarching ideal, as our alleged superiority is itself moral.

Stephen Hare believes that conflicts such as Liddell's disclose the paradox of moral superiority and humility. As Hare sees it, either the individual in question, such as Liddell, knows his moral standards are higher than those of his critics or he does not. If he does not, then he is self-deceived or ignorant, and so much the worse for humility as a virtue. If Liddell does realize that he occupies the moral high ground, then he "cannot fairly subject [himself] to [their] will" (1996: 238). How then can the humble individual retain his humility while asserting his moral values over those with whom he disagrees?

In his refusal to compete on the Sabbath, Liddell clearly refuses to subject himself to the standards of the British Olympic officials, but he does so humbly, with no trace of self-righteousness. How is he able to do this, and do this without any discernible effort? I think that Liddell keeps his apparent moral superiority itself in moral perspective. He does not infer a general moral or spiritual superiority over his detractors because he understands the relatively light moral weight of this one instance of superiority. Moreover, Liddell realizes that God requires more of us than keeping the Sabbath and that the contentious officials might after all be more forgiving, generous, or loving than he.[3]

Liddell also understands that the moral gap between himself and the British officials is insignificant compared to the moral distance between himself and spiritual perfection. As Bernard of Clairvaux remarks, humility makes us gentle (1985: 31). Following Bernard, Liddell's recognition of his own shortcomings surely tempers his reaction to the British officials. The moral ideals of humble individuals are a moderating influence on any favorable comparison they might make between themselves and other people.

The humble individual's appreciation of his fundamental dependence can also be shaping Liddell's gentle attitude toward his peeved countrymen. Liddell feels blessed by God to be able to see the wrongness of competing on His day and to have the fortitude to uphold God's law. The British officials have been under different influences than he, and Liddell understands that not everyone sees things as he does or is as amenable to God's word. In secular terms, we can surely take into account the extent to which other people have missed out on the moral guidance we have received.[4] Consequently, Liddell finds it easy to be gentle with his countrymen and not judge them harshly despite awareness that his refusal to run is more in accord with God's will than their position.

It is also the case that humility promotes patience. Humble individuals do not feel that they deserve special treatment or that others should drop whatever they are doing to attend to the humble person's needs. Waiting for needed attention is not especially burdensome to people who keep their own importance in the proper perspective. So too does humility counsel patience with the mistaken beliefs or contrary values of other people. In this regard, Liddell's gentleness with the British officials may be buttressed with patience; however, it is not obviously or separately displayed in the film-story. In the next chapter, I will address the affinity of patience with humility indirectly, in the context of the impatience to which arrogant people are prone.

Humiliation, humility, and defeat

As noted, the film contrasts the character of Liddell with the other great British runner, Harold Abrahams. The contrasts are telling and varied. For example, the religion of each man is important, but in different ways. Liddell is a Christian missionary who views his running prowess as glorifying God, whereas Abrahams needs to excel to dispel the effects of the anti-Semitism that threaten to suffocate him. Liddell trains joyously and naturally in the Scottish Highlands, while Abrahams opts for highly routinized training in his regimen and technique. But for us, Harold Abrahams is especially important for what he reveals about the difference between being humbled and being humiliated.

On the surface, humiliation and humility are alike. Simone Weil writes that "there is a resemblance between the lower and the higher. Hence... humiliation is an image of humility" (1977: 352). Being humiliated and being humbled both deflate our self-estimation as a result of an unanticipated, untoward experience. Both humiliating and humbling incidents tend to involve psychological dislocation or discomfort as a result of an exposure of our weakness or inadequacy. And the same experience could deepen one person's humility while causing another individual to feel humiliated. However, being humbled and being humiliated differ with regard to self-understanding, and diverge dramatically in the relationship the individual has to himself and to other people.

When Abrahams competes against Liddell in the hundred-meter dash, the stage is set for a thrilling contest of athletes and personalities. The film builds the tension by depicting the two men preparing in their shared dressing room. Appropriately enough, it is Liddell who initiates the honorable exchange of good wishes for the impending duel. The actual race is dramatic and quick. When Abrahams loses to Liddell by a nose, he is crushed. We see him sitting alone in the stands, reliving his defeat, feeling humiliated by it. When joined by his beloved Sybil, he despondently tells her that he does not run to take beatings: "I run to win. I won't run if I can't win." Sybil chides him, saying, "If you don't run, you can't win."

In contrast with Liddell's humility, Abrahams is portrayed as arrogant. Arrogance involves a mistaken, excessive estimation of our worth, either in general or with regard to a particular ability, such as running. From the moment when he takes on the centuries-old tradition of sprinting around the college quadrangle, Abrahams exudes a brazen self-assurance. It is not entirely misplaced, of course, since he is a wonderful runner. But it is nevertheless a failing.

Success and recognition are best accompanied by the humility that is sustained by the moral perspective of which I have spoken. Abraham's experience of humiliation is plausibly viewed as conditioned by his arrogance. As indicated, I will explore arrogance and its harmful repercussions in the next chapter that deals with the exhibition of this vice in the classroom.[5]

The humiliated individual typically becomes angry over his self-exposure. The person feels foolish, but is also irate or resentful over the viewing of his flaws – in Abrahams's case, his lack of perfection as a sprinter. Humiliated individuals are often angry at others, secretly blaming them or circumstances for witnessing their own degradation. Yet Abraham's anger seems focused primarily on himself. Since Abrahams runs to defeat the anti-Semitism that he explicitly calls humiliating, his defeat in the race can be seen as exacerbating the deeper humiliation of his religious discrimination.

In the earlier scene in which Abrahams watched Liddell furiously come from behind to win, he had said that Liddell frightened him; a sign of the fear that underlies Abrahams's cockiness and need for victory as well as a portent of his eventual defeat by Liddell. For Abrahams, anything less than victory, and the excellence that it demonstrates, is failure, and his ego cannot tolerate failure. Abrahams's self-accusation and loathing is therefore prideful, filled with a derision that presupposes self-exaltation.[6] The alteration that accompanies humiliation tends to be only partial and superficial. The individual resolves to avoid letting himself be put in jeopardy, as with Abrahams's impetuously toying with the idea of abandoning competitive running. The humiliated individual is reminded of his precarious place in the world or of his dependence on the fickle opinion of others. His self-evaluation is forced downward and he chafes at his lack of independence. Humiliation motivates the individual to protect himself from looking bad.

And this is exactly the first thought of Abrahams. He resolves to give up running, after only one defeat, and that at the feet of another truly gifted sprinter. Abrahams seeks to protect himself from the pain of failure, of not living up to the expectations he has of himself. But Sybil bucks him up. After saying, "If you don't run you can't win," she tells Abrahams that he can beat Liddell. There is, after all, another way to avoid the humiliation of defeat, and that is to improve. By rethinking his failure and rededicating himself to running, Abrahams now resembles more the person who is humbled than the one who is humiliated.

When humbled by circumstance or by our own behavior, we gain in self-understanding and fittingly lower our self-assessment. The increase in humility gained by this reassessment requires that we be open to recognizing our flaws. And this openness is supplied by the humility that already exists. When humbled, we are grateful for the correction of error in judgment about ourselves. This is why Nancy Snow observes that "humbling experiences...are parts of the educative process of personal growth, maturation, and ongoing development. We learn our limits through humbling experiences" (1995: 214). However, without an existing foundation of humility to begin with, we would be unable to appreciate the real meaning of the deflating experience and this is what happens in humiliation.

In fact, before Lord Lindsay extricates Liddell from his difficulty over running on the Sabbath, Liddell is himself humbled by the conflict. Recall that the refusal to run is the result of Liddell's humility. He cannot put himself and his personal aspirations above the law of God. He is humble before his Creator. However, having to forgo his race further humbles Liddell. He is sorely disappointed at having sacrificed rugby and missionary work to train for three years to compete for Britain in the Olympics only to have that work come to naught. As if he needed the lesson, Liddell is reminded that all of man's planning and labors may be in vain because of God and His place in our lives. Liddell is humbled by having to put his aspirations and work in the larger perspective of God's will.

In contrast with the humiliated person, the humbled individual sees himself more clearly and experiences the disappointing moment as self-edifying. A humbling experience turns us inward. We can be humbled, but not humiliated, without other people being aware of our failing. The humble person has the requisite self-knowledge and perspective to be open to correction. When people are humiliated they have failed to situate their superiority in the moral perspective that governs humility in its fullest expression. When Liddell is humbled by having to defer his plans to God's law, he is not angry. Rather, he is reminded of the place his aspirations have in the larger scheme of things.

Gratitude and god

The film-story also illustrates how the humble person responds to adulation and fame. We should first notice that Liddell does not reject or discount the acclaim he receives. He accepts it, understanding that to avoid recognition is a way of celebrating one's humility.

However, Liddell is neither tempted to dwell on his accomplishments nor to exaggerate them, allures that Richards correctly worries most of us must struggle against. As with Aristotle's truly virtuous person, Liddell is not riven with internal struggle to comport himself in the right way (1962: 200–01, 1152a).[7] Humility comes naturally to him and he is as gracious off the field of competition as he is ungainly on it. Liddell takes his glory in stride because he immediately sees it as an opportunity to promote eternal values and truths. For non-religious people, this would mean using their fame to further such objectively good things as knowledge, community, or fairness.

Just as Liddell has to contend with the importunings of the British officials to run, so he has to deal with his missionary sister urging him to quit running so as to get on with the work of God. She worries that her brother is becoming distracted from their religious work by his running. Liddell passionately answers his sister: "I believe God made me for a [moral] purpose, but He also made me fast." Because he says that God *also* made him fast, running cannot be the purpose for which Liddell believes God made him. Yet his talent for running must also be respected and cultivated as a gift from God, to be used to honor Him. Not to do so, argues Liddell, would be "to hold Him in contempt." It could also be understood as failing to be grateful for a gift bestowed on him by his Creator.

In his response to his sister, Liddell reveals the impartial regard he has for his running ability, as though it belonged to someone else, to anyone. It happens to be God's will that Liddell is fast, so he respects its genuine objective value in the world. Liddell seems humbled before his own talent, just as he would be humbled, for instance, before another person's scientific or musical ability. We must work to develop our own talents for the same reason we would encourage other individuals to develop theirs. As stewards rather than owners of our natural gifts, we have an obligation to cultivate them. Liddell's disinterested treatment of his talents is displayed in the way he pushes his exhausted body to run, as if it were a mechanism for which he has no special regard. Liddell serves God both by developing the talent for running that his Creator has bestowed upon him, and then by using the fruits of that talent (his fame) to gain a wider audience for preaching God's word. The disinterested regard Liddell has for his own talent follows from his recognition of his fundamental dependence on God. Because his running ability is part of God's creation, it is good and Liddell sees himself obliged to develop it.

Is there a secular analogue to regarding our talents and abilities as God-given gifts, developed by us in the service of others? Perhaps. Kant, for example, argues that we have the imperfect duty to develop our talents on the basis of a teleological view of nature and human interest. A system of nature could not be willed in which we disregarded natural gifts; consequently, among our duties to ourselves is the obligation to cultivate our given abilities to be used to achieve all sorts of goals. We do seem to require some overarching moral ideal or vision to invest our talents with a larger social, if not cosmic, purpose. But it certainly seems easier to view our abilities with an impartial eye if we believe in a divine creator than if we lack such belief.

Liddell's story presents belief in God as a strong force for humility in other ways as well. While neither necessary nor sufficient for humility, belief in God gives people a particular being toward whom to be grateful and whose magnificence is itself necessarily humbling.[8] Humble individuals with religious conviction don't have to trace their achievements through a mazy path of dependence on genetic endowment, upbringing, education, and fortunate timing or circumstance. They naturally give credit to God for their abilities and the fortitude to cultivate them.

Forgetting ourselves

Recall Thomas Hill's observation that humility turns our attention to good things in the world, independent of ourselves. This outward focus of humility is figuratively expanded in *Chariots of Fire* through the image of Liddell's ecstatic running. Watching Liddell run with his arms waving, legs pounding, head flung back, and face turned heavenward, he seems transported out of his body even as his body is the vehicle of his ecstasy. Our reaction is cued by the spectators in the film who view Liddell's unworldly running with awed expressions, transfixed by his transfiguration. The fact that this engrossing image is repeated in the film strongly recommends that it be interpreted symbolically. The Scot's rapturous running seems to emblematize the way the most humble of people lose themselves in absorption with what they find valuable in the world.[9] This is a transcendent humility, in which what is independently valuable so dominates attention that we completely forget ourselves. For Liddell, of course, what possesses overriding value is God.

Defending his running against his sister's worry that it will distract him from God and doing God's work, Liddell says, "When

I run, I feel His pleasure." Liddell's experience of being lifted up and out of himself exemplifies the view of Bernard of Clairvaux. Bernard thinks that participation in God's love can lead one "so to forget yourself, that you do not exist, and be totally unconscious of yourself..." (1985: 107).[10] In Liddell's transformation, the diminution in self-awareness that typically characterizes humble individuals culminates in a transient escape from himself. Although Eric Liddell's self-forgetfulness is temporary, it points to the possibility of a devotional humility that could evolve into a permanent transcendence of self.

An individual's loss of self-consciousness might so expand that his personal identity itself is gradually diminished to the vanishing point. If humility presupposes a self to be kept in proper moral perspective, complete transcendence of self would entail, perhaps paradoxically, the eclipse of humility. The process by which humility orients us away from ourselves would thereby culminate in its own demise: the humble person's transcendence of humility through self-transcendence. Of course, such transcendence is merely hinted at in the film's portrayal of Liddell's temporary ecstasy.

Finishing the race

In the character of Eric Liddell, the film provides a paradigm of the man of great accomplishment who nevertheless remains humble. Not only is Liddell fully aware of his exceptional ability, but his humility is never even at issue let alone threatened by his success. I have suggested that Liddell's humility is embedded in a moral perspective that can account for the different aspects of this virtue as depicted in the film. First, Liddell views any success he has in light of his overarching moral/spiritual ideals, ideals which he can never approximate. In addition, Liddell is keenly aware of his fundamental dependence on God for his natural gifts and moral discipline.

The film closes with a reprise of the early scene of the British Olympians running by the ocean. Just as the scene first introduced us to the main characters with close-ups, so do we now take our leave of them, informed by what we know of their challenges and how they deal with them. The faces and bodies of the runners summon up their cinematically rendered histories for us. In the long shot, the flowing line of young men running by the water, dressed in white, resembles nothing so much as a thick ribbon of winding seafoam. Their glory, their youth, even their lives are felt to be ephemeral by virtue of this pictorial association.

Yet we cannot help but think that of all the runners, Liddell has understood how precious our brief time on earth truly is. And that he has understood his place on the team, in the race, and in the world. Liddell has always appreciated the enduring importance of moral ideals and worthwhile undertakings. Whatever success he enjoys has never tempted Liddell to think too highly of himself because his self-understanding has always been situated within his larger moral perspective.

Notes

1 This theme and the rest of the music were composed by Vangelis Papathanassiou.
2 Because our paradigm of humility, Eric Liddell, is a man, when referring to people with humility, I shall take some liberties with what has become the customary practice of balancing gender pronouns.
3 Liddell may also be influenced by another source of sympathetic understanding. He appreciates the motives of the British officials such as their patriotic desire for victory because of his own disappointment at having to throw away three years of arduous practice. Liddell sees how such otherwise admirable motives could sway the officials to compromise their religious compunctions or to be too harsh with Liddell for honoring his.
4 The moral perspective also operates in the regard we have for our virtues independent of moral conflict with others. Luther worries that "true humility, therefore, never knows that it is humble,... for if it knew this, it would turn proud from contemplation of so fine a virtue" (1956: 375). But the humble person who is self-aware need not get carried away with his humility. Not only is he aware of the high degree of humility others have attained and that is required by God or moral perfection, but he realizes how little credit he deserves for whatever level of humility he achieves.
5 There is also a noticeable connection between humiliation and that close cousin of arrogance, vanity. The way in which vanity inclines people toward humiliation rather than being humbled will be investigated in Chapter Six, in the discussion of the film *Young Adult*. The humiliating experience in that film is accompanied by shame.
6 Clearly, I interpret humiliation subjectively. To be humiliated, a person must experience the episode as such. Thus, if I am trounced in a game of tennis, I suffer a humiliating defeat only if I experience myself brought low in the appropriate manner, regardless of the assessment of other people or how it may appear to the public. It is a public, non-subjective matter whether one is belittled or castigated, defeated or denigrated. But whether receiving such treatment results in humiliation is not thereby determined. Of course, in everyday life we do speak of a humiliating defeat or of being humiliated by a tawdry revelation, but this is not the phenomenon to which I refer and it does not correspond to experiences that are, alternatively, humbling.

7 Aristotle distinguishes between the merely continent individual, who must struggle to overcome his baser impulses, and the fully virtuous person who is free of such impulses.
8 I have space here only to indicate the important connection between humility and gratitude. Because they appreciate their radical dependence, humble people naturally feel and express their gratitude. Unlike prideful individuals, people with humility do not mistakenly think they are solely responsible for their achievements. Conversely, acknowledging what we have to be grateful for helps keep ourselves in proper perspective. If I am thankful for my talents and the wherewithal to develop them, I cannot take excessive pride in my accomplishments.
9 I do not mean to imply that Liddell's ecstatic running has significance only for humility or that his character, for that matter, should be interpreted exclusively for what it discloses about humility.
10 Bernard speaks of brief periods of this self-eclipsing state rather than a whole life lived in it. It is this intermittent, temporary loss of self that Liddell illustrates.

Bibliography

Aristotle (1962). *Nicomachean Ethics*, Trans. and Ed. Martin Ostwald. Indianapolis, IN: Library of Liberal Arts.
Bernard of Clairvaux (1985). *The Twelve Steps of Humility and Pride, and on Loving God*, Ed. and Trans. Halcyon C. Backhouse. London: Hodder and Stoughton.
Hare, Stephen (1996). "The Paradox of Moral Humility." *American Philosophical Quarterly*, 33, no. 2, 235–41.
Hill, Thomas (1991). *Autonomy and Self-Respect*. Cambridge: Cambridge University Press.
Luther, Martin (1956). *Luther's Work*, Vol. 21, Trans. and Ed. Jaroslav Pelikan. St. Louis: Concordia Press.
Richards, Norvin (1988). "Is Humility a Virtue?" *American Philosophical Quarterly*, 25, no. 3, 253–59.
Snow, Nancy (1995). "Humility." *Journal of Value Inquiry*, 29, 203–16.
Weil, Simone (1977). *Simone Weil Reader*, Ed. George Panichas. Rhode Island: Moyer Bell Press.

Filmography

Forman, Milos (1984). *Amadeus*, U.S.
Hudson, Hugh (1981). *Chariots of Fire*, U.K.
Reitman, Jason (2011). *Young Adult*, U.S.

2 Arrogance in the classroom
The Prime of Miss Jean Brodie and *Whiplash*

Classroom charisma

Most of us have had at least one teacher over the years who stood out as having made a profound difference in our lives. Film portrayals of such teachers help crystallize for us the qualities that make for pedagogical success in the real world. Besides being intellectually gifted, exemplary instructors keep their focus on their students: listening to what the pupils need and want, asking evocative questions of their students, and offering helpful guidance in understanding the material being taught. In contrast, I will discuss a pair of teachers in the movies who captivate their students but who are ultimately destructive. They are not bad or weak teachers in a conventional sense; they are passionate, knowledgeable, and charismatic. These alluring qualities make them more dangerous than run-of-the-mill or ineffective instructors. Above all, the harmful teachers do not educate as well as they might have because of their arrogance. I have chosen a pair of such cinematic educators: one contemporary and one half a century ago; one male and one female. The flamboyant but destructive teachers are Jean Brodie (*The Prime of Miss Jean Brodie*, Ronald Neame, 1969) and Terence Fletcher (Damien Chazelle's *Whiplash*, 2014).

Jean Brodie (Maggie Smith) is in charge of adolescent girls at a private school in Scotland and Terence Fletcher (J.K. Simmons) teaches jazz at a renowned music school in New York City. Both are passionate about the arts (painting and music, respectively), and genuinely wish to share their passion with their students. Their lack of humility keeps them from being the fine teachers they believe themselves to be and might actually have been. Brodie and Fletcher are egocentric individuals, attuned only to their own views, values, and needs rather than those of their students. The students exist more as a means of self-gratification than as worthwhile in themselves. This arrogance is the basis for their other vices and teaching failures. Because the two are so sure of themselves, they never engage in self-examination or question their teaching methodology, as genuinely excellent movie instructors do. As a result, neither Brodie nor Fletcher truly pays attention to what students think, feel, or appreciate. Instead of eliciting the views or interests of their students, the teachers impose their opinions and tastes on them. Reveling in their considerable authority, Brodie and Fletcher propel students to their death – the most dramatic extreme of their unintentional destructiveness. The varieties of harm they do are painfully ironic, since both see themselves as helping their students to excel.

Arrogance

Arrogant individuals feel superior to other people. They have a dismissive attitude toward the opinion of other, while exalting their own views. Valerie Tiberius and John Walker include the interpersonal dimension of arrogance, noting the arrogant person's haughty treatment of others (1998). The deportment of arrogant individuals exhibits their condescending attitudes and elevated self-regard. For Tiberius and Walker, people who are arrogant believe that they are better than most people because of their accomplishments or station. The arrogant feel a sense of entitlement and corresponding disdain for others on the basis of their possession of "the excellences appropriate to human beings to an above-average degree. They take themselves to be more perfect instances of humanity" (380). As a paradigm of arrogance, the authors cite Mr. Darcy in Jane Austen's *Pride and Prejudice*. Darcy is contemptuous of the character and opinions of those around him because his wealth, education, and intelligence place him so high above them. But Tiberius and Walker view the arrogant person's sense of superiority in strictly non-moral terms: grounded in better breeding or lineage, greater property or accomplishment. Darcy sees himself simply as "a better person according to general standards of what counts as a successful human specimen" (382).

I think they are mistaken by not extending the arrogant person's self-assessment into the moral realm. Tiberius and Walker do find that the arrogant man draws conclusions about his "normative status" in comparison with others, but it is "not (necessarily) that he has more intrinsic moral worth, or more numerous or stronger moral rights" (382). Although Darcy sees himself as a "more excellent human being than those around him, ... he need not think he is therefore more important" (385). But Darcy, along with other arrogant individuals, does think that he is morally more important than those with whom he interacts. As the authors remark about Henry Kissinger, the arrogant individual is convinced that other people should drop what they are doing so as to respond to his demands, and that he should not be bothered with the needs of others and that his interests ought to be given the highest priority. These beliefs, expectations, and demands have a moral basis.

Arrogant people without much thought leap from their technical ability or social advantage to the assumption that they are morally superior to others. The belief in their own "human excellence" that puffs up arrogant people is either equivalent to moral superiority or implies it. Their excessive moral self-evaluation then leads these individuals to "arrogate" rights or privileges to themselves that are not truly theirs. For example, Kissinger believed that "students should consider themselves lucky to see him" (382); and this is precisely the attitude Brodie and Fletcher exhibit in their dealings with their students (and other teachers, in Brodie's case). These teachers pay little attention to what their students need or want, nor do they question their own pedagogical methods. And when things go bad for their students, they do not even entertain the idea that they bear some responsibility for it.

As we saw in the previous chapter, the core of humility is a realistic awareness of our strengths as well as of our limitations. Norvin Richards correctly points out that the absence of self-inflation in humility does not demand a false, denigrated perspective on oneself. For this reason, writes Richards, humility includes an accurate assessment of oneself, coherent enough "to resist temptations to overestimate oneself and one's accomplishments" (1998: 257). However, Brodie and Fletcher do not have such a realistic self-assessment. Instead, they have an overblown, lofty view of their abilities and accomplishments; bad enough in anyone, but especially pernicious in those who are in the business of education.

Humility also disposes us to appreciate and respect what is valuable in a world that exists independent of ourselves. As Sara Ruddick describes it, "Humility is a metaphysical attitude one takes toward a world beyond one's control" (1984: 217). People with humility admire human achievement and natural grandeur; they are humbled by these things. Thomas Hill astutely views humility as "an attitude which measures the importance of things independently of their relation to oneself" (1991: 112). Although Brodie and Fletcher do appreciate the objectively valuable music and painting to which they dedicate themselves, they rarely help their students to hear or see what they find so valuable. In addition, these teachers do not seem to truly value what is objectively worthwhile in their pupils.

The best efforts of the harmful pair of teachers are sabotaged by the vices that are encouraged by arrogance. It never occurs to Fletcher and Brodie to change their teaching methods to better suit their students, because their perception of the students is so thoroughly skewed by their self-absorption. They rarely solicit opinions or judgments of taste from their students, because they only place stock in their own taste, in what is valuable in art (classical painting) and music (jazz), respectively. For both Brodie and Fletcher, teaching is a performance. Interaction with students is more about securing the adulation and power they crave than about encouraging experimentation and discovery. Free to impose their wills on their students, these extremely talented but morally deficient teachers are actually insulated from recognizing failure or taking genuine risk. Though Brodie mouths the (etymologically grounded) idea of education as a leading out, her approach is to put in: to put her ideas and tastes into her girls (who are rendered the "crème de la crème" thereby). She wants to reproduce herself in everyone around her, as emblematized in the portraits painted by her former lover, Teddy Lloyd. All of them bear her likeness, at once humorous and macabre, whether adults, children, or animals!

Both Brodie and Fletcher are striking figures, in behavior and appearance. Brodie carries herself regally, glamorously attired, while Fletcher is dressed in imposing black. Where Brodie airily dismisses views that diverge from her own, Fletcher curtly corrects his young musicians, while making a bicep-bulging fist. The title *Whiplash* explicitly refers to a jazz chart that is played in the film; however, it can also be interpreted as describing Fletcher's pedagogical *modus operandi*: he verbally whiplashes students, demanding to know, for instance, whether the tempo at which they were playing was too slow or too fast, behind or ahead of the correct beat.

The egocentrism of Brodie and Fletcher is revealed in their signature speeches. Brodie generously talks of giving her prime to her girls, reflecting her self-delusion. Fletcher tells of a young Charlie Parker being brutally pushed to greatness, thereby justifying his own brand of trial by fire. They reinforce these speeches with proprietary treatment of the arts to which they are respectively devoted. Brodie haughtily brushes aside a student's opinion of who constitutes the finest painter in favor of an artist whose exalted status seems to be conferred simply as a consequence of being her favorite. Fletcher repeatedly reprimands students by intoning, "Not *my* tempo," as if he owned the beat.

As mesmerizing and inspiring as Fletcher and Brodie are, they are damaging teachers, the more so for their charismatic passion and personalities. Their pedagogical arrogance blinds them to the tastes and needs their students actually have rather than those they distortedly perceive or project.[1] A generous interpretation views the self-absorbed pair as believing that they truly care about their students and are acting for the sake of their education. On this interpretation, Fletcher and Brodie are simply mistaken, unable to see past the exalted conceptions they have of themselves.

Loyalty, authoritarianism, and betrayal

Jean Brodie cuts a dashing figure in the otherwise staid halls of the Marcia Blaine School for Girls in Edinburgh between the two world wars. In her flowing scarves and smartly tailored, colorful dresses, she captivates the girls in her care with a regal bearing, artistic curriculum, and romantic yarns. Each new group of students is greeted with her grandiose self-advertisement, telling the girls that she is dedicated to them, bestowing upon them her prime, and that they are the crème de la crème. Yet we cannot but believe that their status as top-notch students derives from being *her* students rather than from anything special about them.

Because of her unconventional teaching methods and the precocity her girls exhibit, Brodie has a contentious relationship with the dowdy headmistress, Miss McKay. Challenged by the headmistress about her undue influence on the girls, Brodie responds by presenting her pedagogical philosophy, echoing Socrates. She haughtily delivers an etymologically informed lecture on helping students to self-discovery by parsing "education" as a leading out of what is already present ("e" from "ex" as out, and "I lead" from "duco"). Guiding students in their own intellectual quests is part of what Socrates means when he describes his educational work as midwifery (Plato 37, 150D: 1921). The teacher's role as midwife (in prompting students to self-reflection and self-questioning) is amplified upon in Martin Heidegger's conception of the dialectic between teacher and student. He writes:

> Teaching is a giving,... but what is offered in teaching is not the learnable, for the student is merely instructed to take for

himself what he already has… the taking of what one already has is a self-giving and is experienced as such… The most difficult learning is to come to know all the way what we already know.

(1967: 73)

The gifted teacher is able to discern the state of her students' partial, occluded thinking and like a good midwife, facilitate their intellectual labor which results in the birth of greater comprehension or appreciation.

But this is not what we see Brodie doing. Instead, she puts ideas into her students, "intruding" in her words. After all, it takes some humility to subordinate one's own views to the thoughts, talents, and deficiencies of one's students. In contrast, the arrogant teacher seeks to promulgate her own opinions and taste because they are the correct or superior ones. For example, when she asks her pupils who the finest Italian painter is, Brodie brusquely dismisses Leonardo da Vinci as a legitimate response. She proceeds to pronounce Giotto the best. The reason for his superiority seems to be nothing more than: because "he is my favorite." No analysis of what makes Giotto's work superior to Da Vinci's is forthcoming. Brodie then places a Giotto reproduction over a poster of the British Prime Minister Stanley Baldwin which champions safety. Brodie minimizes concern with safety in favor of beauty, or her conception of it. Her rejection of safety will be later inversely echoed by the art teacher Teddy Lloyd and Brodie's former pupil Sandy, when they both tell her that she is dangerous. Brodie puts others at risk, in particular her students, because she is arrogant, elevating her own views above everyone else's.

To be a genuine midwife, to lead out what is present in their students, teachers must first of all be open to their students. Openness entails a kind of attention, one especially alive to the experience of the individuals with whom we are interacting. Nel Noddings portrays the attentiveness needed for caring teaching as "receptive attention" (2002: 15–16). Teachers with this virtue habitually set aside their own interests and preconceptions in order to understand what their students are saying and thinking as well as what they care about. Ideas about what should be taught do not keep these educators from making themselves accessible to their students' tastes and feelings. In the words of Gabriel Marcel, open teachers are "disposable": they make themselves available to their students (Noddings 2002: 18).

Openness needs to be accompanied by responsiveness, a readiness to act on what is perceived as the needs, successes, and problems of the students. The responsive teacher seizes upon what her openness has disclosed to tailor her behavior to her students' perplexities and enthusiasms. Her receptive attention leads to educationally efficacious action. Openness and responsiveness are, therefore, mutually reinforcing. The openness is animated by the readiness to respond to what is perceived; the eagerness to best educate her students motivates the openness. Openness without auxiliary responsiveness would be little more than curiosity or fact-gathering, and responsiveness without openness would be guesswork, as the teacher would have no experiential basis on which to shape her behavior to the concrete demands of the actual students before her.

In contrast to Brodie is the dance instructor (Mrs. Wilkerson) of Billy Elliot, whose love of dance is examined in Chapter Five. In preparation for their improvised duet, Billy's teacher asks him to choose a few meaningful props from his home. She wants her young pupil to create his dance from the material of his own experience, shaping his physical movements according to his emotional life. As a result, Billy includes something from his deceased mother; the dance that unfolds then is a physical leading out from long-stored memories and feelings from within. A paradigmatic example can also be found in a film that is a contemporary of Brodie's tale, *To Sir with Love* (James Clavell, 1967). In this film-story, the novice instructor, Mark Thackeray (Sidney Poitier, also called "Sir") responds to the needs that he observes in his working-class high school students. He jettisons the prepared syllabus and instead offers to talk about anything that interests them in order to prepare them for an adult life that is mature: self-sufficient, personally rewarding, and free of violence.

Brodie is exceptional in ways that do indeed seem to demonstrate a genuine dedication to her girls. She organizes educational field trips, regular tea parties, and excursions to the country estate of her sometime beau Gordon Lowther (Gordon Jackson), the school's music teacher. Luncheon with her quartet outdoors under a spreading tree is a regular feature of the lives of her coterie. There she introduces the girls to such delicacies as *pate de foi gras*, impressing upon them her favorite foods – a complement to her favorite painters, countries, and political leaders. The girls bask in the extra-curricular favors, and readily follow Brodie's lead in the classroom when she substitutes her own artistically skewed agenda for the school's more traditional curriculum. They hang on her every word and thrill to her personal stories of romantic loss and Italian vacations. Her real motivation, however, is to ensure an adoring audience for her performance, one which will perpetuate her views and taste long after the girls graduate from Marcia Blaine.

It is on these unscheduled occasions that Brodie makes her pronouncements concerning the nature and future of her girls: because she is somewhat histrionic, for example, Monica is destined for a career in the theater; Jenny is suited to be a model because of her beauty and a lover because of her natural "instinct"; Sandy's dependability, intelligence, and intuition equip her for a career in espionage. In her next cohort, Brodie singles out Clara for her artistic tendencies. But Sandy chafes at being pigeonholed in such a dogmatic fashion, rebelling against the authority that emanates from Brodie's arrogance.

Sandy rebels against Brodie's high-handed characterizations in two stages: the first personal and the second institutional. Defying Brodie's prognostications about the girls, Sandy usurps Jenny's supposed place as a budding lover. She becomes intimate with Teddy Lloyd, perhaps as Miss Brodie's stand-in, for Lloyd is still smitten with Brodie years after she broke off their amorous relationship. Sandy notices for instance that all of Lloyd's portraits have a Brodiesque cast. She finally ends her own modeling for, and erotic involvement with, the painter when she discovers that he has also insinuated Brodie's features in his portrait of her. Sandy complains, "Even the skin tones are hers." Lloyd laments that he cannot help himself; he does not choose to love Jean Brodie but is "bewitched." Sandy is not placated. As she terminates their artistic and amorous relationship, she notes that being with him is "a waste of time," and that Teddy is really a mediocre painter.

Under a tree, before her next group of girls, Brodie projects her own authoritarian predilections in championing the dictatorial regime of Franco in the Spanish civil war. Even as Brodie's arrogance moves her to certitude and dominance, so does she naturally gravitate to political leaders who seem forceful and seize absolute power. Lloyd has told Sandy that Brodie "invests all leaders with her own romantic vision." This too can be seen as an offshoot of arrogance, a preoccupation with one's own perspective on the world blinding the individual to what is actually there. Earlier, when showing slides of her trip to Italy, she extolled the leadership of Mussolini. Brodie described the fascists as following Il Duce "in noble destiny," but only after describing the dress she had worn at the display of military might! She lauds Mussolini as "the greatest Roman of them all." Arrogance typically manifests itself in the individual assuming more rights or privileges than she has a legitimate claim to. Mirroring the arrogant tyrants she admires, Brodie feels entitled to more of what is socially valued. She "arrogates" to herself more power, attention, or esteem.

As Brodie holds forth about the virtues of Franco, the four former students stop by to listen (Sandy surreptitiously). Brodie explicitly links her own life with that of the dictator, expounding upon Franco dedicating himself to a cause just as she dedicates herself to the girls arrayed before her. Mary McGregor's disclosure that her brother is fighting in Spain prompts Brodie to exhort the girls to be heroines and points out that women can take part in armed battle. Her arrogance keeps Brodie from questioning whether supporting Franco is the right course or whether praising martial heroism to the girls is a good idea. Under the foliage, at her feet, the girls repeat after her that they are "prepared to serve, suffer and sacrifice" for a noble cause. The ever-impressionable, naïve Mary is inspired by Brodie's tribute to Franco and heroism to head to Spain to join her brother in the civil war. But this will now prove to be the captivating teacher's undoing as well as Mary's.

Earlier in the film-story, Miss McKay had pressured Brodie to resign over an overblown but largely accurate letter that Sandy and Jenny had concocted as if it were in Brodie's own hand. The letter purported to be about Brodie's romantic entanglements with both Teddy Lloyd and Gordon Lowther. But Brodie's retort that the writing reflected the imaginative explorations of young girls with budding sexual interests carried the day, forcing McKay to back down. However, Mary's ill-conceived martial expedition results in a tragedy that dooms Brodie's tenure at Marcia Blaine.

Having learned that Mary was killed en route to the Spanish Civil War, Brodie convenes her students, past and present, to inform them of her death. She declaims, "Only I can tell you the truth. Mary McGregor died a heroine." She arrogantly wishes to preempt or replace other descriptions of Mary's tragedy with her own. Brodie then claims that Mary was going to fight for Franco "against the forces of darkness." Although not yet actually fighting, Brodie proclaims that Mary's intentions were noble and heroic, and urges the girls to think of such female luminaries as Joan of Arc and Florence Nightingale along with Mary McGregor. Brodie's account of Mary's death nicely parallels Fletcher's explanation of why a former jazz student of his committed suicide. In both cases, the teachers distort the truth and omit their own responsibility for the former pupil's demise. And in both cases, the truth of their role in the tragedies prompts their removal from the position of authority that they had abused. As Teddy Lloyd had said, people like Brodie are dangerous. When combined with the charm and commanding presence of a Brodie or Fletcher, arrogance can put other individuals, especially young people, at serious risk.

In the climactic showdown between Brodie and the contentious Sandy, Brodie is informed that the tragedy of Mary's death is compounded by the girl's confusion; her brother had been fighting on the side of the Republicans, against Franco! Mary is killed travelling to join the soldiers who were in fact the enemies of her brother. But before Sandy confronts her, Brodie is stunned by Miss McKay's revelation that it is not she but the board of governors who have investigated and demanded that Brodie leave the school immediately. When Brodie protests that she will rely on the loyalty of her girls, McKay trenchantly and confidently calls their loyalty into question. Visibly shaken, Brodie makes her way back to her room, glimpsing the nearby celebration of Lowther's engagement to the attractive chemistry teacher Lockhart.[2]

Back in her own room, Brodie confides to Sandy that she has been dismissed, but that although her students are loyal, "Someone betrayed me, Sandy. Someone spoke against me to the board of governors." It is telling that Brodie and Fletcher as well, both interpret a student's disclosure of the truth about them as a betrayal. It is the language of the person in command, in authority, who has been unjustly sabotaged from within when loyalty is demanded. The reason loyalty is demanded is that the arrogant individual's superiority has a claim on it; the teacher's eminence morally compels her students' support, no matter what. When Brodie babbles on about Jenny's imminent position as Teddy Lloyd's lover, Sandy defiantly announces that it is she not Jenny who is already Lloyd's love interest. After registering surprise at this news, Brodie expresses her bafflement: "I don't understand..." The entire fabric of Brodie's world is unraveling: Sandy as Lloyd's lover, Lowther's engagement, and Brodie's betrayal and dismissal.

Sandy accuses Brodie of causing Mary's death, but Brodie refuses to accept any responsibility for it. Such abdication of moral responsibility seems typical of the arrogant person, yet it also appears inconsistent with feeling superior and wielding power. Shouldn't the individual who is so much better than everyone else and has commanded obedience be just the one to bear the responsibility when things go awry? And yet the inconsistency is only apparent.

The sense of superiority and entitlement includes being above blame or guilt. When Brodie insists that Mary died a heroine, Sandy rejoins that "she died a fool." Sandy points out that Mary was in fact headed toward the wrong army because her brother was actually fighting against Franco and charges Brodie with taking Mary under her wing only because she was so malleable. Brodie realizes the truth then and blurts, "It was you who betrayed me." Sandy retorts, "I didn't betray you. I simply put a stop to you." She adds that Brodie is dangerous and has harmed her, Sandy, by "murdering Mary." It is fair to say that arrogance is at the root of the end Brodie brings about for her student's life as well as for her own career as a teacher. It is fitting that her most perspicacious student precipitates the latter, and this is also the case in *Whiplash*.

Teaching as humiliation

The film opens and closes on aspiring teenage musician Andrew Neyman drumming like his life depended on it. The story focuses on his relationship with the conductor/teacher of the top-tier band in the Shaffer Conservatory, a prestigious music school in New York City. Although not handsome, Terence Fletcher is an imposing figure: his shaved head sits atop an all-black outfit that features a muscle tee-shirt from which he abruptly extends his arms when cutting off the play of his students. As with Brodie, Fletcher spins a favorite narrative that purports to explain and elevate his pedagogical approach and he also constructs a self-serving story to account for the death of a former student. The latter story exalts his role in the student's life, while exonerating him of any responsibility for the boy's tragic end. In the course of his instruction, Fletcher's arrogance mirrors Brodie's in leading him to abuse his position of influence; the result is that he is less effective and edifying than he could have been or that he mistakenly sees himself as being.

Having heard Andrew play a little, Fletcher soon invites him to play with the school's top jazz ensemble, the studio band. When Andrew starts to play, as the backup to the "core" (first-string) drummer, Fletcher nods, smiles, and compliments Andrew. Andrew's satisfaction is short-lived, as Fletcher begins cutting off his play, saying, "Not quite my tempo"; "Downbeat on [line] 18"; "Not quite my tempo"; "All good, no worries." His signature move when interrupting a student's performance is to raise his hand into a foreboding fist as he flexes his exposed bicep. Physical styling accompanies verbal chastising. But there are indeed worries as Fletcher then issues a series of opposite criticisms: "You're rushing"; "Dragging, just a bit"; "Rushing"; "Dragging." The teacher's barked attacks are the verbal whiplash that echoes the title of one of the band's signature numbers (and the film). Having thrown something at Andrew's head, the teacher has Andrew count out the rhythm and slaps the boy's face on the beat to punctuate his interrogative torture. Although Andrew had at first said he did not know whether he was behind or ahead of the beat, he finally blurts, "Rushing," to which Fletcher snarls, "So you do know the difference."

We are as stunned as Andrew at Fletcher's relentless attack, because just minutes before he had had a friendly, supportive chat with his new student in the hall. There, he had asked Andrew whether there were any musicians in his family and had learned that Andrew's father taught high school English and that his mother had left them when Andrew was still a baby. He had also regaled Andrew with his emblematic speech about how Charlie Parker became a great jazz saxophonist, how he became "Bird." The legendary drummer, Jo Jones, threw a cymbal (from his drum set) at Parker for messing up a number, thereby providing Parker with the motivation to practice with sufficient diligence for him to master his instrument. What appears to be about the history of a great jazz musician will be shown to actually be offered by Fletcher as a vindication of his own tyrannical, abusive, pedagogical philosophy. The truly gifted musician will be pushed by Fletcher's brow-beating to his full potential; those who cannot handle his abuse must, by definition, have lacked the talent or intestinal fortitude for the greatness that Parker achieved.

However, the film *has* prepared us for Fletcher's demeaning treatment of Andrew. A few minutes earlier, Andrew had watched him humiliate a trombone player for being out of tune. After ordering Metz to play, he asks him whether he was out of tune. The boy hesitates, stalls in trepidation. Under Fletcher's berating, the trombonist admits to being out of tune. The teacher then orders him out of the room and the band. With a sly grin, Fletcher confides to the group that Metz was not in fact out of tune and that it was another trombonist, "But he didn't know… and that's bad enough." Fletcher views himself as having the right to belittle those under his care because he is the master of his domain. He threatens both Metz and then Andrew with "sabotaging" "his band," the language telling.

Framing a musician's weakness or failure as "sabotage" resonates with Brodie construing an unknown student, then finally Sandy, as "betraying" her. Both terms are in the family of martial language, indicating destruction from within the corps, undermining the intrepid leader's office and campaign. The disloyal soldier sabotages the platoon's operation and thereby betrays the captain's faith in him. The arrogant teacher locates the problem in the disloyalty of the student rather than view the student as flawed or, as in Sandy's case, perhaps justified in finding fault with the teacher. Fletcher's repeated use of possessive language also reflects his overblown self-assessment. Fletcher repeatedly intones: "my band"; "my tempo"; "my [instrumental] part" (merely on "loan" to you); even "my drum set." And all are summed up in "my reputation." The constant expression of ownership and control manifests a license to do whatever the conductor wants, though understood by him to ultimately be in the interests of his charges. Fletcher's harsh words and actions are allegedly justified as the necessary means to winnow the chaff from the real stuff of musicianship. It is ironic that during his hallway, amiable pep talk with Andrew, Fletcher had told him "the key is to relax," adding "have fun." Yet everything in Fletcher's demeanor is designed to keep his players tense and worried about displeasing him or losing their place in the band. The irony is brought home in the following scene of Andrew practicing so intensely that he bleeds, band-aids his bloody hand, and keeps on playing through more blood and band-aids.

In an effort to provide some background for or context for the music and Andrew's fraught relationship with Fletcher, the film provides Andrew with a sketchy romantic interest and a slightly more developed bonding with his father. Throughout Andrew's musical playing and education, his father provides unwavering support. And after Andrew's disastrous termination at Shaffer, it is his father who initiates the process whereby Andrew gives the testimony that results in the end of Fletcher's reign in the school. We will see that Andrew corroborates Fletcher's role in the death of a former student just as Sandy does with regard to Brodie's part in Mary McGregor's demise. Because the real interest of the filmstory is Andrew's drive and interaction with Fletcher, I will elide these peripheral aspects of it.[3]

The arrogant teacher is not truly interested in what his students think or feel; he is too self-absorbed to care about the experience of others. Fletcher never solicits musical preferences or interests from his pupils. Moreover, he never offers much by way of instruction; surprisingly, the band never hears an analysis or commentary of even the jazz pieces they play. In contrast to Fletcher, for example, is Katherine Watson (Julia Roberts) in *Mona Lisa Smile* (Mike

Newell, 2003). She encourages her students to think for themselves and also offers guidance in their art appreciation. Watson shows her students "Carcass," by Soutine – an unsettling side of beef, with intense reds against a dark background – asking, "Is it any good?"; she assures them that there are no wrong answers. The class starts giving their opinions: "It's not art"; "I think it's grotesque"; "There's something aggressive about it, and erotic." One student asks, "Is there a rule against art being grotesque?" Watson also gives help and direction, "Brueghel was a storyteller. Find the stories. Break them down into smaller pieces. You might actually enjoy it." Speaking of Van Gogh, Watson tells her girls that he painted what he felt, not what he saw.

A budding star

Andrew soon displaces the older Tanner as the band's core drummer, but the circumstances cast suspicion on the budding star. Having been handed Tanner's folder with the music for the next piece after the intermission, Andrew has put it down only to have it disappear. When it transpires that Tanner needs the charts for *Whiplash*, and is bereft without them, Andrew chirps that he knows the piece by heart. It looks as though Andrew may have purposely maneuvered to (literally) unseat the first-string drummer. In any event, Andrew is part of the band's victorious playing and becomes the lead drummer. However, Fletcher has another trick up his sleeve. To keep Andrew off-balance, he invites a former bandmate of Andrew's, Connolly, along with the displaced Tanner, to fight Andrew for the choice percussion position. He keeps replacing one after the other, screaming "Motherfucker," and casting aspersions on Andrew's Jewishness, Connolly's Irish background, and Tanner's alleged homosexuality. Fletcher yells repeatedly "Faster," as Andrew drums furiously, bleeding on the drums, until Fletcher at last relents and awards the part to his young protégé. His arrogance encourages the teacher to play his students off one another in a perverse version of competition. Fletcher sees nothing wrong in fostering cut-throat "auditioning" and divisiveness; his exalted self-estimation warrants any ploy that he deems productive of creating the best ensemble.

Recall Bernard of Clairvaux's observation that humility makes us gentle (1985: 31). Awareness of our own limitations and failings inclines us to be forgiving and patient with others. As we would expect, arrogance produces the opposite behaviors. Fletcher is harsh and impatient with his students. His musical superiority apparently justifies him in being brutally demanding, pushing his pupils to meet his standards, on his terms. When their progress is not up to speed, Fletcher becomes frustrated and taunts, shames, or insults them. "Faster," seems to refer to more than the speed of Andrew's drumming; it also includes quickening the pace of meeting Fletcher's expectations.

At the culmination of a harrowing series of events, Andrew's relationship with Fletcher blows apart. The bus the boy is taking to the site of a major competition gets a flat tire; Andrew rents a car and arrives barely in time, but forgets his drum sticks in the car at the rental destination. Although easier to let Andrew play with Connolly's sticks, Fletcher demands that Andrew use his own. Rushing back in the hastily retrieved car, Andrew gets into an auto accident. The upshot is that the disheveled, bloodied boy cannot properly hold onto the sticks as he gamely tries to play during the competition, and is finally told by Fletcher, "You're done." As Fletcher apologizes to the audience for the disaster, Andrew rushes him, tackles him, and begins pummeling his teacher. Band members trundle Andrew offstage while he screeches, "Fuck you, Fletcher. Fuck you." He soon starts to work at a fast food joint, his musical career ended by expulsion from the prestigious school. But his relationship with Fletcher is about to take an unnerving twist, a double twist in fact.

Andrew and his father meet in a well-appointed office with an official-looking woman, apparently an administrator at Shaffer, a lawyer, or both. She informs Andrew that a former student of Fletcher's, Sean Casey, had committed suicide. The mother of the young musician attributes the chronic anxiety and depression that led to her son's suicide to his studying under Fletcher's abrasive tutelage. The woman's lawsuit is not for money, but to stop Fletcher from hurting other students and the school is asking Andrew whether he can corroborate the allegations against Fletcher. As Andrew ponders his decision, we see flashbacks of him putting away his drum kit, throwing out his music tapes, and taking down a photo of his drumming idol Buddy Rich. He is apparently reflecting on these moments as well as a video of himself as a very young boy drumming away. Andrew agrees to sign a statement attesting to Fletcher's anxiety-inducing pedagogical methods.

Andrew (and the audience) had been under the impression that Sean Casey had been killed in a car crash. This was the story told by Fletcher to the band before a practice session: a lie, as Fletcher had been informed that his former student had hanged himself. Although more egregious than Brodie's fanciful evocation of Mary's incipiently heroic death, Fletcher's subsequent embellishment of his relationship with Casey mirrors Brodie's grandiose assessment of her inspirational role in Mary's truncated life. As he plays a tape of Casey playing trumpet, Fletcher spins a self-congratulatory fabrication for his students. He describes the boy as struggling in his second year at Shaffer. Only he, Fletcher, among the conservatory's faculty saw the potential in the "scared, skinny kid. I saw a drive in him and I put him in studio band." After graduating, Fletcher continues, Sean Casey was given a prestigious position in Wynton Marsalis' Lincoln Center orchestra. Appearing to be all choked up, he says that he thought the band should know that "Sean was a beautiful player," and issues a phony apology for his emotional overflow.

Second chance, second confrontation

Sometime later, Andrew stops into a club to hear Fletcher play piano with a jazz combo. Fletcher calls to him as he is leaving and they sit at a table to talk. Andrew acknowledges hearing that Fletcher is no longer at Shaffer but feigns ignorance of his dismissal. Calling him "Andrew" for the first time (instead of "Neyman"), Fletcher confides that he "made enemies," and that parents got a kid, probably from Casey's year, "to say some things about me." Fletcher goes on to vindicate his time at the music school. He says that he does not think people understood what he "was doing at Shaffer... I wasn't there to conduct. I was there to push people beyond what's expected of them... otherwise, we're depriving the world of the next Louis Armstrong, the next Charlie Parker." The invocation of Parker's name primes Fletcher to remind Andrew of his emblematic story of Jo Jones hurling a cymbal at the young saxophonist, thereby goading him to the relentless work required to become great. This time around, Fletcher elaborates upon the edifying yarn by explicitly weaving his own pedagogical aspirations into it.

Andrew quietly wonders, "Is there a line? You know, maybe you go too far and discourage the next Charlie Parker from becoming 'Charlie Parker?'" Fletcher now unveils his self-insulating, foolproof argument. He replies, "No, man. No. Because the next Charlie Parker would never be discouraged." The consequence of Fletcher's reasoning is that harassing and humiliating a musician (whether by throwing a cymbal at his head or screaming at him) cannot be wrongheaded, because if he is discouraged, he never had what it took to begin with! Any student who cannot rise above the denigrating treatment must lack the necessary fortitude, talent, or both. Only the strong thrive! Fletcher's bruising treatment of his students, therefore, is always justified. How tidy and how typical of arrogant individuals. Their inflated sense of self-worth naturally disposes them to alight on scenarios or arguments that support their actions, no matter how destructive in fact. Fletcher concludes by ruing that he never had a Charlie Parker, "But I tried… and I will never apologize for how I tried." The scene features the faces of Fletcher and Andrew bathed in golden light surrounded by darkness, suggesting warm feelings and a reconciliation. Their parting conversation reinforces the optimistic mood. As the pair is leaving the club, Fletcher invites Andrew to play in a competition with his new professional-level band, using material from his old studio ensemble. Andrew seizes on this unanticipated opportunity to redeem himself and reclaim a career in music.

As Andrew settles in with his drum kit on stage with the new jazz players, Fletcher approaches him. Looming above his erstwhile pupil, Fletcher rasps contemptuously, "You think I'm fuckin' stupid? I know it was you [who denounced him to the school]." In retaliation for this betrayal, Fletcher has chosen a new tune, unfamiliar to Andrew, for the ensemble to play. Fletcher offers a sly smile on his way to the podium, relishing the embarrassment about to be visited on the traitor. Thinking that he would be playing the standards from his school days, Andrew is left in the lurch, lacking even the sheet music to try to sight read on the spot.[4]

Andrew tries to fake the number, and various band members chide him as he plays willy-nilly. At the conclusion of the piece, Fletcher sneers triumphantly, "I guess maybe you don't have it." Andrew sits abashed. Befuddled. Ashamed. Fletcher has apparently succeeded in setting him up to fail. But notice that Fletcher was willing to put all the other players at risk by hurting their chances for recognition at the competition, just so he could exact his revenge on the student who "sabotaged" his teaching career. Offstage, Andrew's father gives him a big hug and says, "Let's go home." But Andrew regroups and heads back to the stage. Unlike Charlie Parker, Andrew does not wait a year to demonstrate his musical mastery.

He strides back to the drum set and interrupts Fletcher's address to the audience by commencing to play and announcing the tune to the band, "*Caravan*, I'll cue you." Fletcher is taken aback. Approaching Andrew, he growls, "I'm gonna gouge out your fucking eyes." Andrew plays as if possessed, bringing the whole band enthusiastically along with him. When Fletcher asks him what he is doing, Andrew replies, "I'll cue you," and Fletcher starts nodding and conducting Andrew. Then, just as Fletcher has apparently concluded the piece, Andrew resumes, with an all-out drumming solo. The apparently feel-good ending features Andrew enthralling fellow musicians and audience, and eliciting spirited cooperation from the initially irate Fletcher.

We might thereby conclude that Fletcher's abrasive style has indeed whipped Andrew to greatness. However, there are several aspects of the film-story that indicate the opposite: that the talented boy has triumphed despite Fletcher's imperious and devious manner. First, Andrew's commitment and zest for the music certainly intimate that he did not require manipulation and brow-beating. He plays the drums ferociously, from the opening to closing scenes, even when his intensity bloodies his hands. Fletcher's lying and manipulation are what makes his philosophy and approach suspect. His lie about how former student Sean Casey died is a basis for doubting the rest of his account of his relationship with the student. Fletcher also deceives Andrew about which jazz pieces will be played at the competition, to which the teacher lures the boy he views as betraying him. Indeed, Fletcher is himself willing to "sabotage" the band's performance and the professional prospects of its members for the sake of exacting revenge on Andrew. Then, too, when Andrew returns to the stage and begins playing, Fletcher is not gratified by the success of his demanding, demeaning strategy. On the contrary, he is furious with Andrew and threatens him hyperbolically with eye-gouging. Lastly, Fletcher's strategy, to ruthlessly cull extraordinary musicians from the herd, certainly leaves the less-than-great students in the lurch. They will not learn much from him. The rationalization about producing a jazz giant is more about gratifying Fletcher's ego than about helping students discern greater depths in their music, and in themselves.

Of course, arrogance does not typically issue in such catastrophic damage; however, there is no denying that it can and often does produce harm, sometimes most serious. The arrogant individual's self-absorption is accompanied by the high-handed treatment of other people, treatment that can lead them to do harmful things to themselves. Brodie's and Fletcher's arrogance actually move in opposite directions and are dangerous in contrasting ways. Brodie's lofty flights of rhetoric sweep Mary McGregor up and into harm's way, while Fletcher's mockery and debasing tirades beat Sean Casey down. But even for students that do not come to such extreme grief, the arrogant teacher can fail them in less dramatic and more subtle ways. For example, students are not encouraged to think for themselves, challenge their instructors, or entertain a plurality of views. Moreover, students who are not in Brodie's charmed circle or those who do not shine brightly enough for Fletcher seem to fall by the wayside. Really excellent teachers try to connect with many, if not all, of their students, to help them benefit as much as possible from their classroom experience. That would indeed be using one's prime to the greatest pedagogical advantage, which would include encouraging realistic goals but preclude whiplashing students who falter or do not move at the desirable tempo.

Notes

1 As Iris Murdoch puts it, speaking of love in *The Sovereignty of Good*: "The difficulty is to keep the attention fixed upon the real situation and to prevent it from returning surreptitiously to the self with consolations of self-pity, resentment, fantasy," p. 91.
2 When informed earlier of the couple's engagement, Brodie's arrogance impelled her to lie, telling Lloyd that she had herself instigated Lowther's advances on Miss Lockhart.
3 It should be noted that Andrew himself is guilty of a bit of arrogance. At the dinner table, he pooh-poohs his cousin's football accomplishments while asserting his own musical ambitions and he breaks off his budding romance on the grounds that his girlfriend would want him to forgo practicing his drums if he continued with seeing her.
4 The story line here is a bit confusing, for it implies that Andrew never even practiced with the band before the competition. But perhaps in practice sessions in which Andrew did participate, they only rehearsed the pieces with which he was familiar.

Bibliography

Bernard of Clairvaux (1985). *The Twelve Steps of Humility and Pride, and on Loving God*, Ed. and Trans. Halcyon C. Backhouse. London: Hodder and Stoughton.

Heidegger, Martin (1967). *What Is a Thing*, Trans. W.B. Barton and Vera Deutsch. Chicago: Henry Regnery.

Hill, Thomas (1991). *Autonomy and Self-Respect.* Cambridge: Cambridge University Press.

Murdoch, Iris (1971). *The Sovereignty of Good.* New York: Schocken Books.

Noddings, Nel (2002). *Starting at Home.* Berkeley: University of California Press.

Plato (1921). *Theatetus*, Trans. Harold Fowler. Cambridge, MA: Harvard University Press.
Richards, Norvin (1988). "Is Humility a Virtue?" *American Philosophical Quarterly*, 25, no. 3, 253–59.
Ruddick, Sara (1984). "Maternal Thinking." *Mothering*, Ed. Joyce Trebilcot, 213–30. Totowa, NJ: Rowman and Allanfield.
Tiberius, Valerie and John Walker (1998). "Arrogance." *American Philosophical Quarterly*, 35, 379–90.

Filmography

Chazelle, Damien (2014). *Whiplash*, U.S.
Clavelle, James (1967). *To Sir with Love*, U.K.
Daldry, Stephen (2000). *Billy Elliot*, U.K.
Neame, Ronald (1969). *The Prime of Miss Jean Brodie*, U.K.
Newell, Mike (2003). *Mona Lisa Smile*, U.S.

3 Art and integrity in *The Fabulous Baker Boys*

Virtue and talent

When we first meet the Baker boys, they are not so fabulous anymore, nor are they any longer boys – in any sense. Their two-piano lounge act is looking somewhat time-worn, as are they. We get the impression that the act's popularity has been declining for awhile. The older brother, Frank (Beau Bridges), doubling as the pair's manager, suggests adding a female singer. Susie Diamond (Michelle Pfeiffer) does inject needed pizzazz into their performance, yet she is ironically placed. Even as the attractive singer revives the almost moribund act, she precipitates its unraveling. Susie forces Jack (Jeff Bridges), the more talented younger brother, to confront his reluctance to strike out on his own as a bona fide jazz pianist.

As it follows the trajectory of the rebounding and final fraying of the Baker brothers' musical fortunes, *The Fabulous Baker Boys* (Steve Kloves, 1989) explores a variety of topics. These include sibling love and conflict, art and artistry, and simply surviving in a tough world. Woven through this dense fabric of issues are questions of virtue. In my view, the dominant virtue that is scrutinized is integrity, augmented by two auxiliary strengths of character: courage and honesty. Integrity marks an individual whose self is a coherent, consistent whole. Important aspects of the individual's personality reinforce one another rather than being disparate or in conflict. Gabriele Taylor and Raimond Gaita argue that the person with integrity is one "who keeps his self 'intact', whose life is 'of a piece', whose self is whole and integrated" (1981: 143). The person with integrity acts in ways that express his or her important values, interests and commitments; someone who lacks integrity does not live up to her principles or what supposedly matters most to her. In what follows, I will explain how *The Fabulous Baker Boys* is a story about reclaiming one's integrity.

There is no particular behavior that is naturally or practically associated with being a person of integrity, the way, say, giving something of value characterizes generosity or waiting calmly typifies the person of patience. Any action, taken as a discrete item out of the context of the individual's values, may demonstrate integrity or exhibit its absence. As such, integrity is a second-order moral trait, supervening upon the work of the virtues that govern and direct everyday action.[1] Here is how integrity differs from the standard virtues that may be roughly divided into the substantive and executive. Integrity differs from substantive virtues such as justice that supply the individual with specific ends or goals. When people champion justice, their actions may then be judged as possessing or lacking integrity, depending on whether the actions promote this ideal. However, people for whom justice is not a high priority do not lack integrity when they ignore it; they might, of course, be faulted on other moral grounds. It follows then that integrity itself is "empty"; as Bernard Williams explains, "It is not a disposition which itself yields motivations, as generosity and benevolence do...." (1981: 49).[2]

Integrity is also unlike such executive strengths as temperance or diligence, which enable individuals to withstand temptations of desire or emotion in order to do what is consonant with what they value most. This can include achieving the goals or purposes provided by substantive virtues. As such, these executive virtues, which include patience and fortitude, are also associated with the exercise of will power.[3] Integrity is unlike these virtues of will power, in that it does not help fight off motives or interests that compete with doing what moral or non-moral values call for. Integrity is maintained when the first-order virtues function so as to keep the person intact, harmonizing the various aspects of his or her personality into a relatively integrated whole.

The integrity scrutinized by the film is Jack's, calling into question the younger brother's fidelity to his considerable musical talent. Late in the story we learn that he despises performing the standard musical fare with his brother, night after night, year after year, and that he really wants to be creative and play jazz. Taylor and Gaita argue that following through on one's commitments is necessary to keeping oneself whole and intact – to living with integrity (1981: 144–46). Early on we see Jack playing piano with nuance and controlled passion at a jazz club, without his brother. We infer that he does so infrequently. The reason Jack lacks integrity is that his commitment to his art is half-hearted; he cannot make the leap of faith – in himself. He knows that he hates the lounge act, is moved by jazz, and has talent. On some level, therefore, Jack also knows (though he tries to hide it from himself) that he owes it to himself to give himself fully to the music he loves, however risky this may be. The arc of the film-story can be viewed as Jack coming to face his lack of integrity and deciding to do something about it.

Talent would seem, on the face of it, to be tangential or irrelevant to integrity. This is because integrity is typically about being true to, integrated with, one's moral principles values. Although integrity is a moral virtue, the commitment in question need not itself be a moral one. There are two ways the moral virtue of integrity can be relevant to one's non-moral talents or gifts: one broadly, involving the talent; the other more strictly, as explicitly fulfilling a moral duty. First, integrity can apply more broadly to concerns outside the moral sphere. It can encompass worthwhile dimensions of the self, such as intellectual, physical, or artistic abilities, including playing the piano. Insofar as integrity is a virtue that addresses the self as an organic, unified entity, it can speak to an individual's relation to his or her natural abilities. How we relate to non-moral aspects of ourselves can therefore have moral significance. Fulfilling our potential by realizing our talents, I shall argue, is a significant aspect of Emerson's moral perfectionism – his version of living the good, complete, or "true" life.[4]

As indicated, for Taylor and Gaita, the pivotal relation of the person to his or her abilities is one of commitment. Jack hides his true passion beneath the schlock routine with his brother, allowing it only sporadic and inadequate expression. He refuses to commit to a riskier and more demanding life style out of fear of failure. Commitment requires courage, because sticking to that which we most deeply value may be risky. The second way in which integrity can be relevant to talents is via the moral route espoused by Kant. Kant argues that we have a moral obligation, an "imperfect duty," to develop at least some of our natural gifts (1959: 40–41). On this view, integrity can be found more narrowly in carrying out one's moral duties to oneself. Imperfect moral duties involve acting in ways that further or promote humanity in others and ourselves. Developing our natural, albeit non-moral, abilities is an important respect in which we promote our own humanity. Once an individual recognizes his talents and understands his moral obligations to himself, if he knowingly "lets his talents rust," then he would be betraying his integrity. He cannot maintain his moral wholeness if he disregards this fundamental dimension of self-development.

John Kekes has a view of integrity that articulates commitment in such a way as to further clarify Jack's lack of it. Kekes divides integrity into two components: principled action (authenticity) and constancy. Constancy is "wholeness," acting according to a life pattern that one has deliberately chosen (1983: 499). It is this latter dimension of integrity that pertains to Jack. Effort may be needed for constancy because the pattern one has chosen may conflict with "some external authority, one's pleasure or security, the temptations of wealth, power, or status, or the inherent difficulties involved in adhering to the pattern" (501). Jack's moral weakness involves both the creation of and adherence to the pattern of which Kekes speaks. First, the pattern of living the life of a jazz musician is hazy, for Jack has not thought it through in much detail or with much clarity. It is something like an inarticulate vision. Second, Jack makes but fitful, unsystematic attempts to live in accordance with the pattern: playing jazz now and then, in private or in the local black jazz club. Apropos of Kekes' remarks, the ideal life that Jack unreflectively hankers for conflicts with the security and money he derives from teaming up with his brother. Then, too, there are "inherent difficulties involved in adhering to the pattern."

Integrity often requires courage as well as honesty about oneself. Both have an important bearing on Jack's crisis of integrity. Courage is needed for integrity when acting on our moral principles or our non-moral commitments can put us at risk.[5] Standing up to injustice, for instance, can jeopardize one's friendships, livelihood, or even life itself. In the case of being true to such natural abilities as intellectual prowess or artistic talent, we must risk failure. In *Good Will Hunting* (Gus Van Sant, 1998), fear of failure seems to hold Will back from pursuing his impressive mathematical gift.

Individuals may not maintain the integrity sustained by moral action or talent cultivation because they feel safer in refusing to put themselves to the moral or technical test. In their confrontational scene, Susie does in fact accuse Jack of cowardice, because he allows his fear of musical failure to keep him stuck in the numbing rut of the Baker Boys' humdrum routine. To some extent, Jack's lack of integrity is due to what Taylor and Gaita identify as a weakness of will. He is not true to his quasi-commitment to serious music, and often "...acts on reasons which in his own view are insufficient reasons for acting" (1981: 146). The insufficient reasons are those which motivate Jack to remain teamed up with his brother. Among his reasons, however, may also be the more salutary one of looking out for his less talented brother, who has the responsibilities of a family and mortgage. On his own, true view, he has "overriding reasons for acting otherwise" – to devote himself to jazz. On Stanley Cavell's interpretation of Emersonian perfectionism, Jack is not meeting "the demand for providing reasons for [his] conduct, for the justification of [his] life" (2004: 24).

Honesty is a companion of integrity whenever courage is demanded for it. We naturally gravitate to ways of deceiving ourselves in rationalizing inaction, when acting with integrity is difficult or dangerous. For example, we might tell ourselves that the injustice we perceive is not real or is not so great as to call for our involvement at this time. Honesty about what our moral principles or convictions truly require of us is then an indispensable auxiliary to integrity. In the case of talents, such as Jack's musical gift or Will's mathematical genius, we need to be honest about their presence and importance to us; otherwise, the individual can pretend that he is not truly gifted or that the talent itself is not, after all, terribly meaningful. When our lack of integrity is confirmed by our not being true to ourselves (in our morality or ability), honesty is then needed to understand the various ways in which we have avoided recognizing our lack of harmony as a person. The confrontation with Susie and a subsequent humiliation of the brothers' act finally force Jack to be honest with himself and his brother. He gives voice to his frustration with the act and with himself, finally acknowledging his lack of integrity and the price he has paid for it.

Here I should distinguish two modes of integrity-dereliction. The first is as I have been describing Jack: the person who does not in his behavior honor his commitments, uphold his principles or try to promote what he values. Yet there is another sort of failed integrity, more radical than the typical kind exemplified by Jack. This is the defect besetting individuals who are so utterly lacking in commitment, principle or value that integrity cannot even be a live option for them. Such people opportunistically pursue whatever seems attractive, pleasant or apparently in their interest with no thought about its bearing on something deeper to which they have tethered themselves – because that deeper bedrock of value is missing. As such, they are unmoored and integrity is logically beyond the reach of the unmoored. We should then distinguish between those who are capable of integrity because possessing the requisite value-laden underpinnings but do not attain or sustain it, from those individuals whose emptiness precludes them from even attempting to act with integrity.

Jack has felt miserable playing with his brother for most of his adult life. Compromising his musical gifts has nagged at him throughout, making him surly. We sometimes speak of artistic individuals as "prostituting" themselves or their art when they sell out their talent: the would-be serious novelist who pens pulp fiction; the talented painter who does magazine illustrations; the song writer who creates commercial jingles. When people who are capable of artistically (or intellectually) worthwhile activities forgo them to merely make a buck by pleasing others, we often criticize them for wasting their talent, or at least giving it short shrift. Like the literal prostitute, Jack puts himself at the disposal of customers and their taste, instead of doing what he truly deems worthwhile. For Emerson, this is a species of the conformity that keeps us from becoming who we truly are.

Jack's brother, Frank, has no problem carrying on with the duo's act because he is a limited musician; endlessly playing songs like "Feelings" suits him just fine. But Jack chafes, primarily because he has not taken the real chance that his musicianship demands. Emerson provides an astute diagnosis of Jack's discontent: "A man is relieved and gay when he has put his heart into his work and done his best; but what he has said or done otherwise shall give him no peace" (1993: 24). Consequently, Jack suffers – existentially, down to his core.

Taylor and Gaita observe that integrity can keep people from acting in certain ways; for them to follow a particular course of action would make them "fall apart" (1981: 156). Violating a deeply held principle, or not following through on a commitment, would undermine the integration of self, setting the person of character adrift. The position of Taylor and Gaita makes it seem as though integrity is an all or nothing matter: the individual either acts with integrity and keeps it together or acts contrary to his commitments and falls apart. The character of Jack in *The Fabulous Baker Boys* portrays someone who is explicitly struggling with his integrity, which is shown to be a matter of degree, as with most if not all virtues and vices.

Jack can be interpreted, in retrospect, as someone whose eroded integrity is eating at him because he cannot fully commit to deploying and developing his gifts. The film then adds an important dimension to our understanding of integrity. It depicts an individual who lacks integrity, but whose growing self-awareness of this lack moves him to radically change his life. By implication, we can infer that another sort of person could come to Jack's self-understanding but still resign himself to a safe path, continuing to compromise his integrity despite its psychic toll. The mechanism employed to bring about such resignation is likely to be some sort of rationalization, one that would have to be accompanied by self-deception or another mode of dishonesty.

The aloofness with which Jack is portrayed throughout much of the film can be viewed as a lack of energy, resulting from the bland music the brothers play, or, more dramatically, as a defense mechanism to mask his unwillingness to embrace his natural talent. The hostility he occasionally shows his brother, and later Susie when she talks of leaving the act, seems, after all, to arise from his being at odds with himself. After Jack leaves his brother in order (at last) to be a serious pianist, Jack's previous angry outbursts now strike us more clearly as venting his dissatisfaction and disappointment with himself for how long it has taken him to try to live up to his considerable ability. He suffers from being dishonest and cowardly with himself. For example, when mid-story Susie rhetorically asks, "You're good, aren't you?" Jack minimizes his ability, saying "I can carry a tune." The false modesty is not so much a clumsy expression of humility as a way to avoid the truth and the high-stakes decision it would all but force on Jack.

The trouble with Jack

The first three scenes of the movie provide a window into Jack's life and a glimpse of his soul. The film opens with him leaving a woman he's shared a bed with. Dressing in a tuxedo for the evening gig with his brother, Jack says, "Funny job," in response to the woman's "Funny hours." When she asks, "Will I see you again?" Jack replies, "No." Blunt but honest. A one-night stand. The scene prepares us for Jack's essential isolation, and his callous response to even a hint of enduring intimacy. For much of the movie, Jack appears detached and sardonic. As he is leaving, the casual sex partner tells him that he has great hands: the dexterity of piano playing translated into love-making. The allure of his touch will serve Jack well later in the film-story, with another paramour.

We next see Jack onstage with his brother Frank for the act that the pair have been doing for fifteen years. Frank does the warm-up of corny patter as Jack taciturnly looks on. When getting paid by the lounge manager, Frank inquires about future bookings. The manager, Lloyd, coldly repeats, "I'll call you." Jack tells his brother to count the money in the proffered envelope and says "Fuck him," in response to Frank complaining about Jack's attitude. The manager's behavior suggests that the Fabulous Baker Boys are not doing so well, a hint that is soon confirmed by the owner of another club. But we also see Jack's hostility, played off against his brother's *bonhomie*, which borders on obsequiousness.

Cut to Jack smoking, to strains of a girl playing "Jingle Bells" on the piano in his apartment. She is at Jack's place because her mother "has a new friend." Jack has slept on the couch in his clothes. The girl chats amiably as she brings him a cup of coffee, and Jack asks about Nina's mother's boyfriends. She folds a blanket as they talk and then deftly exits out Jack's window and up the fire escape to her own apartment. The brief episode conveys Jack's easy familiarity with the girl, indicating that he is something of a surrogate uncle for his young neighbor. It also displays Jack's gentler, caring side. His capacity for uncomplicated, unromantic affection will be reinforced in his relationship with his dog. In fact, the film-story is built on Jack's various relationships.

Foremost, of course, is Jack's relationship with Frank, and the music they play to earn a living. But Jack also has a closeted attachment to jazz music, an inspiring connection that is in glaring contrast with Jack's distaste for the popular fare he and his brother routinely grind out. The other ongoing personal relationships involve Nina and his hound. What shakes things up is Susie Diamond, the singer the brothers recruit to breathe some life into their stagnating act. Jack's relationship with Susie, personal and professional, gives the movie and Jack's life their energy and beauty. It also exposes fissures in the bond between the brothers, and pushes Jack toward honesty and self-knowledge.

The four relationships involving Jack ground the narrative arc of the story. The arc curves toward three highly charged episodes: two confrontations following a consummation. The consummation is between Jack and Susie, and the confrontations involve Jack and Susie, and then Jack and his brother. These pivotal interactions and the relationships that inform them define the plot; how the protagonist deals with his brother and Susie (and the music in his life) flesh out and give meaning to the events in the film-story. Undergirding the characters and their interactions is the formal structure of the film. The climactic episodes grow out of incidents that are enlivened by repetition and reversal. These formal features give the film a sturdy structure. As with music itself, repeating and reversing salient features of preceding events give the film a rhythmic form that buttresses its narrative content.

New blood

We soon see Frank and Jack playing in a cheesy Hawaiian setting, in loud tropical shirts, for a sparse and uninterested crowd. The club owner, much warmer than the earlier lounge manager, pays them for the night they perform as well as the next night. He tells the brothers that they are a class act but perhaps he and they need "a vacation" from one another. To Jack's curdled remark that this is the first time they have been "paid off," i.e. paid not to play, Frank suggests they take on a singer and says, "Two pianos isn't enough anymore." Ever laconic, Jack replies, "Never was."

The auditions that follow are both funny and poignant. The first woman sings "Candy Man" terribly. Frank tries to stop her, but Jack devilishly keeps accompanying her, prolonging the excruciating performance. The film then offers quick takes of the next brace of singers, providing a lively telescoping of a series of enthusiastic flops. Afterward, Frank notes that not one of the thirty-seven women they had heard could carry a tune. Ever detached, Jack humorously quips that "there was a certain surreal quality to it." Through the low rent, dusty space, cluttered with tables and chairs, a straggler stumbles in, mumbling, "Damn it. Shit," because the heel of her shoe has broken. Frank informs her that the auditions are over and, like a schoolmarm, points out the importance of punctuality. After protesting not being given a chance, Susie Diamond delivers a telling blow, "So, where's the winner?" The line not only gains her the audition, but it shows us that she is both clever and quick. The brothers perk up when she sings "More Than You Know"; she puts her gum back in her mouth when done and says, "So?"

On her first night, Susie starts off shakily: struggling with the microphone and dropping the crib notes for her songs. The boys demonstrate their professionalism by improvising, and Susie slides in beautifully as if it had all been planned. That's all we see of her debut. After the show, Frank berates Susie for unwittingly saying "Fucking" when the mike went back on. He then admonishes her not to take tips. Susie quickly rejoins, "Then I want my picture on the poster [outside the club]." At the next performance, Susie looks polished and the joint is packed. A slow pan discloses the poster on which Susie's photo and name are larger than those of the Baker Boys, indicating where the group's newfound drawing power is coming from.

When the brothers are getting paid, again by Lloyd, the film offers the first of many repetitions. The formerly disdainful manager now asks if he can sign them for next week, to which Jack sneers,

"We'll call you." Repeating the phrase "call you," Jack also reverses the earlier exchange during which Lloyd had snidely told the musicians that he would call them in response to Frank's inquiry about future booking. A visit by Jack to a black jazz club will also be repeated, twice. During the first visit, Jack discusses the playing of a young pianist with Henry, the owner of the club. Subsequent scenes at the club show Jack more involved, playing the music he cares about.

The two least complicated of Jack's relationships, with his dog and neighbor girl Nina, come together in a short Christmas Eve scene. Jack brings his dog home from the veterinarian, following an after-hours argument with the uncooperative young clerk, and finds Nina making herself at home in his apartment. Jack brings over an alcoholic drink for himself and eggnog for the girl, and tells her that she can stay the night even if her mother comes home alone. It may be a bit of a cliché to illustrate Jack's sweet side with a dog and a neglected child, but the matter-of-fact way Jack behaves gives the relationships credibility. Moreover, the contrast with the complex relationships Jack has with his brother and Susie is well-placed dramatically. In fact, Jack brings his dog with them on their trip to a luxurious resort where they are booked.

Susie is excited by the prospect of the hotel's glamour as portrayed in its brochure and Frank's skepticism is shown to be misplaced when the place lives up to its promise. She next cracks wise, humorously commenting on the gift baskets of fruit awaiting them in their suite: "Looks like Carmen Miranda had an accident in my room," alluding to the lively singer of a bygone era who performed with an impressive fruit arrangement atop her head. The crowd loves them and the trio celebrates on their terrace, drinking champagne. It is a happy, relaxed moment. A little tipsy, Frank tells Susie that his brother is brilliant: for remembering all their venues with corresponding dates and for his feel for music. When Frank suggests that Jack dance with her, Susie archly says, "I think your little brother prefers to dance alone," jabbing at his aloof demeanor. But they do dance, dreamily, on the balcony. Susie backs away from a potential kiss, taken aback at her own reaction to Jack. Something is obviously brewing between the two attractive but hard-boiled loners, who are wary of emotional entanglement.

Jack and Susie share a quiet, unanticipated moment the next morning. Walking through the deserted main floor of the hotel, Susie hears Jack softly playing jazz beautifully, alone in a side lounge. She smiles with delight, enters the room, and leans on the piano.

She has discovered Jack's talent. Jack playing jazz will also be reprised in two later scenes. Frank sees them and looks a little apprehensive, as if realizing that he is a third wheel. His nervousness carries over into the next scene, when his complaining about Jack's smoking is revealed as displacing his real concern that Jack will get sexually involved with the winsome Susie and jeopardize their act. Back in their room, the Baker brothers will soon blame each other for their piano playing being out of sync. The bickering turns into a food fight, recalling an earlier incident and presaging a much more serious display of violence: another of the repetitions that give the narrative content formal scaffolding. However, the sexual electricity generated during the balcony dance between Susie and Jack crackles as the camera shows them apart, but clearly thinking about one another.

Consummation

The job at the fancy resort builds to an entwined consummation of Jack's professional and personal relationships with Susie. Frank's departure for a domestic emergency leaves Jack and Susie alone, on stage and off. On stage, Jack and Susie deliver a stunning rendition of "Makin' Whoopee" for New Year's Eve. It is a showstopper, for us watching the film as well as for their enrapt audience. Unencumbered by his brother's pedestrian piano playing, Jack complements Susie's sensual singing with understated elegance on the keyboard. Susie reclines on top of the piano in a slinky red dress, slithers and flirts with Jack. Instead of playing the straight man to Frank's brand of folksy palaver, Jack reacts to Susie's sultry performance with a wry, knowing smile as he accompanies her in a silky, modulated style. It is obvious that the attractive couple could be more successful without Frank. Teaming with Susie, Jack could even find room to do some improvisational playing, incorporating his proclivity for jazz into their act.[6]

After the New Year's Eve countdown and the audience has left, Susie whispers something in Jack's ear and kisses him. She says, "You're good, aren't you?" Jack deflects the compliment and Susie talks about her life in the escort service business. She makes herself vulnerable by opening up, remarking that staying in nice rooms did not really change her life. Jack listens quietly, but does not disclose anything personal in turn. Jack massages Susie's neck. We may recall from the opening scene with the one-night stand that Jack has "great hands." He caresses Susie, kisses her neck, massages her back. Susie swoons and groans, "Oh, shit," at melting under Jack's ministrations. They kiss.

In the morning, Jack stealthily leaves their shared bed, mirroring his leave-taking from that earlier carnal encounter with the stranger. Susie clearly wants something more than Jack seems able or willing to give. She will soon break up with the brothers, perhaps in an attempt to force Jack to self-examination and authenticity. Back in town, Susie walks up to Jack's apartment and is taken aback when Nina opens the door, but no words are exchanged, at least on screen. She goes to "Henry's," the neighborhood jazz club, and finds Jack playing with understated artistry, with a black combo. Reenacting her discovery of Jack's jazz proficiency at the hotel, Susie listens appreciatively but surreptitiously to him play, then slips away and awaits him at his apartment door. Jack bestows a half smile on her and they go inside. After sex, Susie prepares to leave while Jack sleeps, reversing Jack's previous post-coital departures (from Susie and the initial sex partner). Before she can exit, however, Nina pops in through the fire escape window to walk the dog.

When Jack joins her in the living room, Susie tells him the reason she came by was to let him know that she was thinking of leaving the act. Someone in the audience at the posh New Year's Eve job had suggested she sing in a cat food commercial. Jack says, simply, "Take it." Surprised, Susie grunts, "Huh?" and points out that she is "just thinking about it." Jack repeats his brusque, "Take it." Susie looks disappointed at Jack's unwillingness to put up a fight – to keep her in the act and in his life. As if to remain tied to the Baker brothers, Susie reminds Jack that Frank has the trio booked through March. Jack reassures her not to worry and brushes off her asking about how he feels about her leaving, dismissively adding, "There's always another girl." But this scene is just a warm-up to the cutting confrontation between Jack and Susie that soon occurs.

Confrontation

After the next evening's performance, Susie scurries after a departing Jack. She informs him that she has told Frank she is quitting. Jack's terse, "Congratulations," elicits from Susie a fierce, "As of now." Susie obviously has feelings for Jack, maybe even Frank. When Jack sarcastically offers to give her a recommendation, Susie says, "Jesus you're cold. You're like a fucking razor blade." Jack offers another pointedly placed repetition of something Susie had earlier said to him when he had made a friendly overture: "Careful, you're gonna have me thinking you're going soft on me." He then asks her if she wants him to beg her to stay and (mistakenly) claims that the Baker boys can survive without her. Jack's refusal to acknowledge that he needs Susie, on and off the stage, blatantly exposes his pride. He cannot bring himself to admit this vulnerability or Susie's value to him. Jack's pride will emerge again, with a vengeance, during his parallel showdown with his brother.

Susie then cuts to the heart of Jack's existential conflict. She tells him that she was at the jazz club the previous night, and saw him "dusting off his dreams." She continues, "I was there. I saw it in your face. You're full of shit. You're a fake. Every time you walk into some shitty daiquiri hut [to play with his brother] you're selling yourself on the cheap." Susie confesses that it mirrors her own, earlier self-deception with regard to her dealings with men in the escort service. In response to Jack's cutting remark that he did not know "whores were so philosophical," she snaps, "At least my brother's not my pimp." Susie crisply sums up the notion that we can prostitute ourselves by selling out our talent and aspirations. Accusing Jack of cowardice, she connects his dishonoring his ability with fear of failure. It can indeed require courage to put our talent to the test; by avoiding the possibility that our abilities may be inadequate, we protect ourselves from emotional harm.

In criticizing Jack for being false to himself, Susie fulfills the Emersonian office of the "friend," albeit in a rough-edged confrontational manner. In the words of Stanley Cavell, the friend "instigates" and "accompanies" us on our journey of becoming who we truly are (2004: 27). In particular, the friend encourages us in that central task of moral perfection of making us intelligible to ourselves and to others (26). Susie is insightfully articulating the fulcrum upon which such intelligibility turns: "the demand for providing reasons for one's conduct, for the justification of one's life" (24). It is as if Susie is pleading with Jack to heed Emerson's call to an "aversion to conformity," in order to free himself for the journey of developing and expressing his considerable musical talent (1993: 26). So much of Jack's life has been spent, unhappily, on stage with his brother in a soul-bruising compromise that he has lost sight of who he is (Cavell 2004: 22–23).[7]

Here Jack passes up the opportunity to point out the irony in Susie's accurate analysis and criticism of him. First, Susie was herself literally a prostitute. But more to the issue at hand, she certainly seems to be prostituting her own talent by singing in commercials instead of working with musical charts whose creative arrangements demand that she develop as a serious singer. Jack may be too stunned by the truth of Susie's diagnosis of his condition or he might simply not wish to make such an obvious comeback to her charge of prostitution. Either way, Susie has the last word, and Jack is at a standstill, staring at her hurrying away.[8]

How exactly does the prostitution metaphor apply to "selling out" our talents? Literal prostitutes put their bodies at the service of other people. Their sexual activities are determined from without, extrinsically, by the interests and desires of customers – anyone who can pay the necessary fee. Sexual prostitutes subordinate their own desire for physical and emotional intimacy to making money. Their sexual interactions are thereby dictated from without, by what John Kekes calls "external goods" such as money, status, and respect (1983: 506–07). Instead of forfeiting control of their bodies to clients, prostitutes could choose partners on the basis of their own personal preferences, from within. Entering into sexual relationships because of one's own taste then is to make these choices from intrinsic reasons, reasons internal to the action and to one's self.

Now consider the struggling writer. Instead of penning advertising copy, she could be composing old-fashioned sonnets or new-fangled experimental fiction. When she writes the advertising, she puts her talent at the disposal of the desires and interests of other individuals, those who will pay for her services. In just this way, Jack subjugates his musical talent in order to serve the imperatives of popular taste in the brothers' lounge act. When Jack plays the jazz he loves, his piano playing is determined from within, intrinsically. His desires and passions are intrinsic to what he plays and how he plays it. The resultant goods are what Kekes considers internal: they are "self-developed... they come to a person... as a result of his inner lifer... The satisfaction is part of having done well" (1983: 507). This sense of intrinsic direction (self-determination) is tied to another: the talent is now intrinsically, essentially connected to the nature of the medium. Playing music that one finds worthwhile necessarily engages the pianist with the challenges and opportunities inherent in the art: relationships among notes, chords, harmonies, dissonances, rhythms, and tempos.

By acting in his own true interests, therefore, a gifted individual will naturally develop his talents (satisfying an imperfect, Kantian, duty to the self). Dealing with the demands of the medium will call forth artistic growth. The individual will delight in the growth itself as well as in the more developed product of his increased artistry.

Such internal goods moreover are inseparable from the ideal pattern that is the basis for constancy, the second dimension of Kekes's integrity, "Internal goods are constitutive of an ideal pattern" (1983: 507).[9] Championing his brand of moral perfection, Emerson exhorts: "Insist on yourself; never imitate. Your own gift you can present every moment with the cumulative force of a whole life's cultivation" (1993: 44). To spend one's talents simply for the sake of external or extrinsic goods, as Jack has been doing, lacks integrity because it cannot be realizing an ideal pattern. Just as Emerson warns, living this way has made Jack "false in all particulars" (28).

Frank, however, is not lacking in integrity or prostituting himself. He seems quite content to exercise his limited talent playing what the crowd wants to hear (it beats giving piano lessons to suburban kids). Frank's insistence that the trio have an "obligation" to play the likes of songs such as "Feelings" suggests that he has internalized the popular taste, making the extrinsic interests of the paying customers his own. The character of Frank shows that not everyone who uses his abilities to achieve extrinsic aims prostitutes his talent and thereby lacks integrity.

Fraternal fracas

The troubled relationship between the brothers finally erupts in a verbal and physical confrontation. It is precipitated by a disastrous appearance on a late night, or early morning, telethon. The telethon fiasco had been preceded by sagging, indifferent audiences for their now singer-less act. Not only is their spot on the telethon at three in the morning, on an obscure cable channel, but the cause is merely to raise money for a local gymnasium. As if this were not bad enough, the emcee gets their name wrong and then interrupts their number to crow about the contribution results. The altercation between the brothers follows upon Jack blowing up at the emcee and scuffling with a telethon organizer. Distraught with Frank for arranging their demeaning appearance on the shabby show, he growls, "We were always small time, but we were never clowns." Jack's pride has been pricked and Frank seems impervious.

Pride seems to occupy an ambivalent relationship to integrity. On the one hand, pride can compromise integrity. Pride can keep us from being true to ourselves because doing so can risk failure. Because I do not want to threaten the high regard I have for myself, I avoid the requisite display and scrutiny of my talent. I can keep my pride aloft, therefore, by not exposing myself to coming up short. But that avoidance necessarily undermines my integrity because I am not giving myself a chance to realize my full potential. On the other hand, pride in our ability can push us into giving ourselves the chance to shine. Playing easy-listening tunes in daiquiri joints or obscure telethons finally is too much of an affront to Jack's pride in his musicianship. Feeling debased is part of the impetus for him to exit the piano tandem and enter into the more complex but dicey world of jazz.

Of course, the ensuing shouting and fighting are the culmination of more than this humiliation or even the floundering of the act. For years, Jack has been frustrated, sticking with it because of a combination of forces. As I have been arguing, besides loyalty to his brother and simple inertia, Jack was reluctant to see whether he had what it takes to play demanding jazz. Jack could also be using his support of Frank, who has serious financial family obligations, as a rationalization for not trying to play serious music on his own. Jack is likely more angry with himself than with Frank – for remaining in a job that he admits to loathing. The burden of staying with such work is exacerbated by his awareness at some level that he should strike out in a more fulfilling direction. The scene also fits firmly into the film's underlying formal structure of repetitions and reversals. It is but the last and most violent in a series of acrimonious interactions that become physical. Early on, Jack cuffs Frank for fussing with his appearance before a performance, having warned his older brother to stop. Later, in their room at the fancy resort, angry words give way to a food fight. The repetition and escalation of physical conflict unobtrusively prepare us for the concluding sibling combat.

After Jack has lashed out at his brother for having no pride, Frank lectures Jack about taking responsibility for getting sexual with Susie and destroying the act. Frank finally shoves Jack into a fence. Jack tries to stop the fighting, but when Frank plows into him again, Jack spins Frank around and bangs him into the fence. The struggle ends with Jack ripping, symbolically, at Frank's fingers and groaning, "I'm through with it. I can't do it anymore."

For the Baker brothers, music can no longer mediate their relationship, and the hostility is chronic because the music they share is commensurate with Frank's modest talents, but not with Jack's ability and true aspirations. We soon see Jack playing again at Henry's jazz club, and Henry offering him a slot on Tuesdays and Thursdays. This is the third time we see Jack playing the music about which he is passionate and also the third time we see him in Henry's. These are crucial repetitions because of the importance of jazz to Jack and the genuine opportunity Henry's represents for him.

Jack eventually makes his way to his brother's home to explain himself, in an effort to salvage their relationship. Frank mistakenly thinks that his brother has come to reestablish their act, but Jack sets him straight by finally owning up to the truth. He confesses that every night they played together, from the moment he was on stage, he could not "wait for it to end." Adding, "I've been lying to myself long enough," Jack indirectly connects honesty with integrity by intimating that lack of honesty dovetails with his failure in integrity. The Baker boys share a drink from a commemorative bottle of liquor pictured in an early photo of their act, face each other at a pair of pianos, and play a song from that period in their career. A rapprochement, or its beginning, has been affected, and Jack, uncharacteristically, took the initiative.

He continues to do so by showing up outside a building from which Susie emerges, likely her apartment building. Jack brings up "the other night," referring to their angry parting of the ways. They both blurt, "I was out of line." When Susie asks if the brothers have found another girl, Jack sheds his armor and tells her that he did not look. Besides referring literally to the act, this could also indicate that Susie is the one for him. In addition to the reversal of Jack going to Susie, where before she had come to his digs, the film ends with a one-two punch of linguistic reversal and repetition. When Jack asks Susie, "Will I see you again?," he harkens back to the film's opening scene of the-morning-after. Only this time, it is Jack, not the woman, who inquires about continuing the relationship. Susie asks him what he thinks, and he responds by quoting her line from the audition episode, saying that his "intuition" tells him that he will see her again.

The concluding reversal and repetition resonate with their numerous predecessors: Jack's repeated jazz playing and reversal of the manager's "I'll call you"; the reprising of fraternal fighting and Susie adopting Jack's bedroom exits; and Susie duplicating Jack's artistic prostitution even as she throws his nasty barb about being a whore back at him. These are the structural underpinnings of the narrative substance of the film – Jack's important relationships with people, music, and his dog. Jack's positive relationships with his neighbor girl and dog persist, although he has had to apologize to Nina for snapping at her. Jack has severed his working relationship with Frank, but has made a good faith effort to repair their friendship. In closing out the Fabulous Baker Boys, Jack has also freed himself to explore a career in jazz.

No longer playing jazz intermittently, Jack now has a regular spot in the schedule at Henry's club. Who knows what will happen with Susie, whether she will resume a personal involvement with Jack or even form a professional duo with him. Whatever happens with her, Jack has allowed himself to be vulnerable, open to intimacy. Most importantly, Jack has clarified and strengthened his relationship with himself. Honestly facing his deepest desire, Jack has remedied his lack of courage by going all in on his impressive musical talent. Committing himself to the music he loves is the foundation for Jack to begin to meet the demands of the virtue of integrity. Emerson crystallizes Jack's realization and resolve this way; "Nothing is at last sacred but the integrity of your own mind" (1993: 26).

Notes

1 Integrity resembles humility in being a second-order virtue that concerns the self. Unlike humility, however, integrity does not address the self directly or in as such a straightforward manner.
2 This is not to say that integrity could never function as a motivation. However, to act for the sake of one's integrity would provide a purpose or end that may be of questionable virtue. It implies too much conscious regard for one's moral purity, a form of "self-indulgence," to use Williams's term. Instead of being overtly or directly concerned with their integrity, people should focus on acting in ways that uphold their core values and purposes; when they do so, integrity takes care of itself.
3 For a helpful discussion of these two types of virtue, see Roberts (1984, 224–47).
4 The importance of developing and exercising one's natural gifts to integrity is a major reason why standard dictionary definitions of the virtue are incomplete. For example, although a definition of integrity as being honest and having strong moral principles points in the right direction, it does not take into account the bearing of integrity on fidelity to oneself in ways that are not blatantly ethical. As such, it misses the relevance of Emersonian perfectionism which, I shall suggest, is aptly proposed as an elaboration of integrity. I would also note that the honesty that is crucial to integrity chiefly concerns oneself and is not honesty *simpliciter*.
5 Kekes uses the extended example of Callisthenes' defiance of Alexander the Great's demand for formal obeisance to show that constancy can involve great risk. Although Kekes does not explicitly laud the courage of Callisthenes, he (Callisthenes) exhibits it in order to maintain the life pattern to which he has committed himself, a pattern that would have been fractured had Callisthenes bowed down to Alexander.
6 Roger Ebert offers this appreciative observation of the scene: "Whatever she's doing while she performs that song isn't merely singing; it's whatever Rita Hayworth did in *Gilda* and Marilyn Monroe did in *Some Like it Hot*, and I didn't want her to stop." "The Fabulous Baker Boys," October 13, 1989: rogerebert.com/reviews/the-fabulous-baker-boys-1989.

7 For Cavell and Emerson, the literally "false position" Jack has assumed on stage means "settling too soon for the world as it is" and has "obscured" him to himself; see Cavell (2004: 22–23).
8 We might suspect the film of giving Susie too much credit for philosophical or psychological insight in her dissection of Jack's life. In an effort to explain Jack to the audience, Susie may seem to be playing the role of the detective in movie mysteries who unravels the criminal's motives and methods to other characters (and audience). But Susie has demonstrated considerable street smarts by asking, when she is late for the audition, "So, who won"; demanding her picture on the poster; discerning Jack's musicianship; and criticizing venue bookings. Moreover, the colloquial style in which she expresses herself is consonant with her movie persona, lending credibility to her thoughtful analysis of Jack. We could, then, be permitted to give her the benefit of the doubt when it comes to holding a mirror up to Jack.
9 The internal or intrinsic goods can result from all sorts of life plans. Besides the intellectual and artistic pursuits Kekes and I dwell on, individuals can derive intrinsic value from a range of careers: from engineer to brick layer, from surgeon to hospital receptionist, from high school teacher to farmer. We can also find intrinsic satisfaction in other efforts, such as rearing children, maintaining a household, or playing a worthwhile part in community organizations.

Bibliography

Cavell, Stanley (2004). *Cities of Words: Pedagogical Letters on a Register of the Moral Life*. Cambridge, MA: Harvard University Press.

Ebert, Roger (1989). "The Fabulous Baker Boys." rogerebert.com/reviews/the-fabulous-baker-boys.

Emerson, Ralph Waldo (1993). *Emerson's Essays: First and Second Series* ("Self-Reliance"). New York: Gramercy Books.

Kant, Immanuel (1959). *Foundations of the Metaphysics of Morals and What Is Enlightenment?*, Trans. Lewis W. Beck. New York: Macmillan.

Kekes, John (1983). "Constancy and Purity." *Mind*, 92, 499–518.

Roberts, Robert C. (1984). "Will Power and the Virtues." *Philosophical Review*, 93, 224–47.

Taylor, G. and Raymond Gaita (1981). "Integrity." *Proceedings of the Aristotelian Society*, Supp. Vol., 143–59.

Williams, Bernard (1981). *Moral Luck*. Cambridge: Cambridge University Press.

Filmography

Kloves, Steve (1989). *The Fabulous Baker Boys*, U.S.
Van Sant, Gus (1998). *Good Will Hunting*, U.S.
Vidor, Charles (1946). *Gilda*, U.S.
Wilder, Billy (1959). *Some Like It Hot*, U.S.

4 *Amadeus* as a portrait of envy

A complex portrait

The film *Amadeus* (Milos Forman, 1984) opens with a scene of a wintry night, whose chill air is pierced by the loud cry of "Mozart," and then "Forgive me, Mozart" in an anguished voice. The invocation of the great composer's name comes from Antonio Salieri, who is soon rushed to a hospital after apparently trying to kill himself. The tortured venting of Mozart's name not only sets the tone of the film, it encapsulates the narrator's attitude toward his rival: haunted by conflicting emotions of reverence and admiration, revulsion and resentment. As the story unfolds, we see that Salieri understood and adored Mozart's music as no one else could, with the possible exception of the genius himself. But Salieri was also consumed by envy for the composer's unmatched musical gifts. The film pulses with the tension between Salieri's unqualified love of Mozart's music and absolute loathing of its creator. To the extent it can be, this struggle is resolved through the awful gnawing of his envy. Although Salieri's envy is seemingly straightforward, the film reveals complexities and depths in this most self-wounding of vices. The portrait of envy that emerges from the film-story incorporates the following dimensions: types of envy; existential seriousness; the axis of humility-arrogance; proximity; and destructiveness.

Envy is doubly personal. Its objects are people, people we know. We envy them their possessions, but our envy is based in feelings we have about ourselves. Consequently, although envy looks outwardly, away from ourselves, it is a self-centered virtue. It is centered on the self in that the individual must have certain feelings about him or herself in order for envy to arise. We must view ourselves as deficient and feel deprived. We lack something we value and chafe at our lack. Typically, we keep envy private, aware that it is a blemish on our character. Understanding his envy as a damning trait, Salieri waits until the end of his life to confess it. What we see on the screen, the entire film, can be understood as a portrayal of Salieri's self-disclosure to a young priest who has come to minister to him in the hospital/asylum to which Salieri has been confined for decades. To do this, the film establishes a rhythm, punctuating Salieri talking to the priest in the present with flashbacks that depict what the aged man is purportedly recalling but not explicitly narrating. The confession reveals an apparent self-awareness that is often elusive in the case of envy because the vice can distract us from ourselves. Envy turns our attention on its object: the thing we covet and the person who enjoys it. I say that the self-awareness is "apparent" because we do not know how reliable a narrator Salieri is, after all. How much of what he says or we see is self-serving, mitigating the older composer's consuming envy?

The type of envy found in the depiction of Salieri is malignant, harmful to the person who is afflicted with it as well as others. Yet not all envy is vicious. John Rawls notes that some envy is benign, as when we "remark upon the enviable harmony and happiness of a marriage" (1999: 308). Here we are expressing without rancor how much we value what this couple enjoys. If we told the pair that we did indeed envy them their connubial bliss, they "would be expected to receive [the remarks] as a kind of praise" (308). Feeling this way about the possession of another person (or couple) is not a vice; it is rather a positive evaluation amplified by the wish to have the good thing in question. Such benign envy can sometimes morph into the more practical form of emulative envy: an appraisal and feeling that "leads us to try to achieve what others have" (308). With emulative envy, the attitude functions to motivate us to act in ways that we believe and hope may secure for us the good thing that we value and see others enjoy. Envy that is of the vicious sort does not operate in such a straightforward or beneficial manner.

What makes envy malignant is the animosity we bear toward the person who possesses the valued object that we wish we had. We resent the individual for having the wealth, talent, station, or status we covet, and would like to see her deprived of it. We wish the fortunate individual harm, especially if the harm meant the loss of the thing we cherish. Vicious envy admits of variations. In what Gabriele Taylor calls "primitive envy," we view the person who has the prized object as actually responsible for our lack of it. As she points out:

> The other, as the possessor of the good, is seen, rightly or wrongly, as somehow causally responsible for the deficiency in the life of the person envying him: it is because the other has it that it is not available to her.
>
> (1988: 236)

We are deprived of the chairmanship of the Philosophy Department because Jones was given the position instead of us. As a consequence of Smith inheriting the bulk of grandmother's estate, we must scrape by. But the envy Salieri feels toward Mozart is not of the primitive sort, at least not directly. Salieri does not lack the exceptional compositional powers that Mozart possesses because Mozart has them. Rather, it is God's fault for bestowing the musical genius on Mozart instead of Salieri. For Salieri, it is as if God had to choose between them and selecting Mozart as the beneficiary of His largesse is what has left Salieri in the lurch, as the inferior composer. So, besides his hostility toward Mozart, Salieri is also angry at God. Salieri's envy could then be understood to be an indirect species of primitive envy: as the beneficiary of God's gift, Mozart thereby cheats Salieri of musical brilliance.

Taylor also articulates a form of envy she calls "sophisticated envy." Unlike primitive envy, the person suffering the sophisticated strain does not view the other person's possession of the good things as "responsible for our lack of them, but rather for out being seen to lack them" (1988: 236). The complaint in sophisticated envy then is that the person with the desirable object or trait makes us look bad by comparison. Taylor explains that the exposure of our deficiency may be to others, ourselves, or both. "His courage, effectiveness, and cleverness can hardly be the cause of her lacking them, but they may be the cause of showing her and the world that she does lack them" (1988: 236). Salieri sees that, over time, Mozart is (properly) viewed as the finer composer, becoming more popular as his own renown fades. Salieri does suffer from sophisticated envy due to the disparity between Mozart's enduring popularity and the waning attention his own music receives.

Nevertheless, Salieri is not predominantly animated by the difference in how the world sees his and Mozart's abilities and their fruits. Taylor remarks that the person in the grip of sophisticated envy need not actually prize the object or attribute in question (1988: 237). S/he might merely wish the high regard that attaches to its possession, as in the case of receiving an honor or being looked up to as royalty or nobility. And this certainly is not Salieri's problem. He does not esteem himself less merely because other people praise Mozart; rather, he does truly value music and the talent to create music at the highest level. Nevertheless, there is an aspect of Taylor's analysis that pertains to Salieri, an aspect of "being seen." The "seeing" in question, however, is Salieri's own; it is self-reflexive seeing.

Mozart makes Salieri see *himself* as deficient. Before Mozart comes on the scene in Vienna, Salieri basks in the approval of the emperor, his retinue of musical officials, and the musical public. Only when astonished by the beauty of Mozart's creations is Salieri confronted by the truth about himself – that he is second rate. As Iago remarks about Cassio in Shakespeare's *Othello*, "He [Cassio] hath a daily beauty in his life that makes me ugly" (1954: 867; Act V, Scene I). Salieri's self-esteem suffers in his own eyes. Salieri is not without talent, it is simply not at the dazzling height of Mozart's. So when Salieri is heralded as the finest composer by the emperor after Mozart has been working in Vienna for some time, the praise rings hollow. Lesser ears than Salieri's may find him terrific, but the court composer knows with certainty that Mozart is without peer.

The character of Salieri embodies the way in which envy is chronic and painful. To the pain of deprivation is added the bite of its shamefulness; we are naturally plagued by the unsavoriness of this vice. Consequently, envy all but demands rationalization: a justification to lessen the moral and concomitant psychological burden it imposes. Typically, a moral belief grounds the narrative we construct to enable us to view our envy as warranted. The narrative accounts for why in fact we deserve the coveted object, either *simpliciter* or more than the person who actually possesses it. Rawls' view of how we might address our feeling resentment can be applied as well to envy. He thinks that when feeling resentment, we must believe that "their being better off is the result of unjust institutions, or wrongful conduct on their part" (1999: 308). According to Rawls, we may think our lack and the other's enjoyment of the desirable object is the result of an injustice done to us. And it is incumbent upon us to offer an account or narrative to vindicate our harsh response to the person who has the object of desire. Salieri embraces a form of this reasoning, but the "institution" in question is none other than God.

In his own defense, Salieri offers Mozart's debased character as the reason for resenting his receipt of such magnificent musical gifts from God. If the vulgar, lascivious, immature young man we see is refracted through Salieri's psyche, then we rightly conjecture that he is likely exaggerating Mozart's flaws in order to buttress the permissibility of his own splenetic moral stain. In Salieri's judgment, he is a more moral person than Mozart and so more entitled to God's bounty. Where Mozart is common and coarse, Salieri is reserved and refined. Where Mozart yields to his baser lusts, Salieri restrains himself out of respect for women. Where Mozart is boastful and brash with his superiors, Salieri is deferential. Salieri realizes that he is ultimately challenging God by questioning His judgment. He is tortured by the fittingness of Mozart's middle name, "Amadeus"; the man is truly beloved by God. But he should not be.

But why could Salieri not simply accept that Mozart is the finer composer? We certainly do not envy everyone who has something we wish we had. Often we just experience Rawls' admiration envy and look up to this woman's intellectual or athletic prowess, or that man's computer skill or handsome face. Here the film-story suggests competing hypotheses. One is that it is a matter of ego, pure and simple. We want the good thing for ourselves and resent another person just because he has it. Why shouldn't it be me? We then cast about for a way to justify us in feeling resentment. The moral superiority Salieri offers, then functions merely to excuse his wretched vice. However, the belief in his moral superiority to Mozart might be crucial to Salieri's envy. On this hypothesis, and it seems to be the one that Salieri wants the priest (or us) to buy into, Salieri would not be envious were Mozart morally worthy. He would then have been free to delight in Mozart's music, befriend him, and promote his career. I do not think that the film does or can resolve this ambiguity for us. Instead, it prompts us to reflect on the dual place that a justificatory account can occupy in relation to envy and the difficulty in adjudicating between the two in real life cases.

Music is not just central to Salieri. It is his overwhelming passion, his *raison d'etre*. If we believe his self-report, there is nothing that even occupies second place in his priorities. Appreciation of the overarching value of music to Salieri leads us to see that the object of envy admits of degrees of what we might call existential seriousness, depending upon how much the desirable object is valued and how firmly it is entrenched in our deepest selves. Consider envying a coworker her better position in the work place. If it is simply status, as in Taylor's sophisticated envy, it would seem fairly shallow and not terribly grounded in who we most truly are or aspire to be. It would not have much existential seriousness. Similarly with coveting another person's spouse. Perhaps having this person for our own would improve our lives, but not in the most fundamental of ways.

But if we envied a fellow worker her position because having it would provide the opportunity to realize our most important ends, to most fulfill our potential, well that would seem to be existentially vital. So what? What difference does degree of existential seriousness make? The idea is that the most existentially serious sort of envy makes the suffering more poignant and makes a sympathetic attitude at least somewhat reasonable. Should the person who enjoys what we value trivialize or waste it, our envy is now supported by something like righteous indignation. A politician who barely beats us out for a powerful office is using it to simply line his pockets where we would have tried to promote public welfare. It is to Salieri's credit, then, that the good he values is essential to his life, so much so that he does not try to minimize Mozart's genius. We feel for Salieri because nothing would have given him greater joy than to have reached such heights of musicianship. Then, too, he cannot disparage Mozart for somehow misusing or wasting his talents, the way he could with someone who took easy routes to popularity or squandered his gifts simply on making money.[1]

Loving the music, loathing the man

As mentioned, the bulk of the film-story can reasonably be seen as Salieri's confession to the young priest who is visiting him in the hospital. The priest has heard that Salieri (F. Murray Abraham) has accused himself of killing Mozart – the tease that strings us along until the film's finale. When Salieri first espies Mozart (Tom Hulce) at the Prince Archbishop of Salzburg's Vienna place, he does not realize that the goofy, playful young man who is lasciviously jesting with an attractive young lady is indeed the musical prodigy. From his concealed place, Salieri hears a giddy Mozart talking backwards to romantic and scatological effect with Constanze Weber (Elizabeth Berridge), soon to be his fiancée and then wife. Salieri is then amazed and appalled to discover that the young man who had been crawling around the floor playing with the woman with striking décolletage is indeed the celebrated artist who is now conducting the performance of one of his compositions for the Archbishop and his guests down the hall. He tells the priest, "That night changed my life." He recalls the music, "An oboe, A single note, hanging there, unwavering. Until a clarinet took it over, sweetened it into a phrase of such delight," closing his eyes in rapture. Salieri still feels the exquisite beauty of the buffoon's celestial composition, suggesting that he can replay every note of everything he has ever heard of Mozart's. He explains, "This was a music I had never heard," and describes the "unfulfilled longing" as "the voice of God." Salieri is plagued by God's decision to give this wonderful talent to such an oaf, an "obscene child."

As if to contrast Mozart's talent with Salieri's, we soon hear Emperor Joseph (Jeffrey Jones) play a short march that Salieri has written to welcome Mozart. When the emperor subsequently offers the sheet music to Mozart as a memento of the occasion, Mozart demurs, claiming that "It's already in my head." Joseph demands a demonstration. Mozart plays it from memory flawlessly, ungraciously offers a critique of it, and proceeds to suggest improvements. His concluding guffaw seems to simultaneously scoff at the piece and point to his own mastery. Needless to say, Salieri is taken aback at Mozart's brashness as well as his undeniable facility. Mozart's genius, on display in his own work and his rendering of Salieri's, shows Salieri his limitations, heretofore hidden from him amidst the sustained acclaim with which his own compositions have been met.

Compounding Mozart's lack of social grace and tact is his financial profligacy. As a result, his wife "Stanzi" secretly brings one of her husband's compositions to Salieri in the hopes that he will recommend Mozart for the position of musical tutor for the emperor's niece. The composer himself is too proud to make such a supplication by submitting samples of his music in an open competition for the royal appointment. The soundtrack conveys the music Salieri hears as he reads the original drafts, amazed that Mozart had no need of revision, simply "taking dictation" as the young composer wrote down what was already complete in his head. Salieri's facial expression masterfully captures the torture of his conflicted reaction of ecstasy and despair. The power of the music transports the lesser composer and thereby immediately arouses his despair of ever achieving his heart's desire: to create at this superb level. Salieri is mesmerized. Spellbound. Enthralled. Entranced. He does not need an orchestra. His musical mind translates the written notations into the most remarkable sounds he has ever imagined. Salieri drops the heap of sheet music and walks out of the room, stunned into silence. He resolves to undermine Mozart's fortunes whenever he can and thereby thwart the God who has given this undeserving, loutish brat these fabulous gifts.

The film calls attention to another important moral trait that intersects with envy, namely the axis of humility-arrogance. Were Salieri more humble about his own moral character, he would necessarily be less judgmental about Mozart's. The moral superiority he feels toward Mozart fuels his envy by giving him moral grounds to feel slighted. Salieri's lack of humility, moreover, even extends to God. He elevates himself above God, judging Him to have made a mistake in showering His blessings upon this imp. How dare God favor Mozart over him! Now surely, for a God-fearing man such as Salieri has understood himself to be, such judgment is hubris in the service of blasphemy. Greater humility about his own moral virtue would have served as a curb on Salieri's envy. Recall from Chapter One the ways in which humility tends to augment other virtues. For example, Nancy Snow's observation that humility is a force for compassion and forgiveness toward others (1995: 211). And Bernard of Clairvaux explaining how acknowledging our own flaws and limitations, essential to humility, disposes us to being merciful and gentle with other people (1985: 31). Greater humility might well have freed Salieri to admire and praise Mozart unalloyed with hostility. Salieri could then have befriended the young man and championed his music. And yet, Mozart's character and behavior encouraged Salieri's envy, at least to the extent that the version of Mozart he presents (to the priest and us) is accurate, and it is likely to be distorted so as to favor the narrator.

What we see is an arrogant man who flaunts his prowess and invites resentment through his own lack of humility. Mozart bridles at criticism and bristles at being questioned in his choice of libretti for operas. He shows off shamelessly, as with playing Salieri's march, and refuses to demean himself by competing for the position of tutor to the emperor's niece. When Salieri praises *The Marriage of Figaro*, Mozart cannot resist replying, "Of course, it's the best opera yet written." Although his behavior and the lack of virtue it manifests do not justify envy, they certainly make it more understandable. They afford a basis on which Salieri can mount the rationalization for his hostility toward Mozart (and God). The humility-arrogance axis then intersects with envy from the standpoint of the object of envy as well as the person with the vice. For contrast, Michael Cassio does not give Iago similar grounds for his envy. Cassio is neither boastful nor mean-spirited as Mozart clearly is. Iago can tell himself that he is more deserving of the promotion that Cassio has received, but cannot invoke Cassio's character to do so, as Salieri has done with regard to Mozart.

We have seen Mozart drinking a good deal as he composes and at the parties that he frequents. Now we watch him saunter along the Viennese way, taking swigs from a bottle of booze as he enjoys the hurly-burly and mini-performances of life on the street. Mozart jauntily takes in food stalls, a dog performing by running on a large ball, a man eating fire, a bear walking upright on a leash, and groups of horses, chickens, and soldiers: the bustling activities echoing his drink-laced mood while affording him commonplace material later perhaps incorporated in an opera, enriching the score and libretto with textured detail. The man who can make such beautiful music is also jeopardizing his talent by making merry, a bit too much. Disciplined and inspired, Mozart is also dissipated and irresponsible. Because all his time is occupied with composing and carousing, Stanzi soon leaves him, taking their little boy with her to another town.

But before that happens, on this day of carefree strolling, Mozart's father visits the young couple unannounced. Although an imposing figure, in black cloak and stern expression, his son is overjoyed to see him. Wolfgang is more embarrassed than intimidated, and so feels the need to cover up for Stanzi's indolent housekeeping as well as the couple's financial straits. Leopold clearly disapproves of his son's penchant for drink and revelry, and the lack of income which pupils would provide. In addition, he had belatedly cautioned the boy not to marry so young, and now urges him to return home to Salzburg. Nevertheless, Mozart spirits Leopold off to a masque ball where a disguised Salieri requests that Mozart play something by him. Mozart obliges, playing in an ape-like fashion and finishes the mocking tribute by bending over and farting. Salieri is obviously offended by Mozart's public sport at his expense. The scene offers a madcap blend of Mozart's superciliousness with his vulgarity. In retaliation, Salieri soon sends a young woman to work as a maid for the Mozarts, a spy in the guise of a gift.

The support and attention Mozart's father has lavished upon him add another layer to Salieri's envy. Where Leopold has been unstinting in nurturing his son's outsized musical ability, Salieri's own father had disdained his son's parallel ambitions. Seeing no practical value in music, he had claimed that a performing child would be displayed like a pet monkey. Having prayed to God to be a great composer, Salieri takes it as a miracle when his father chokes to death, freeing him to eventually make his way to Vienna, the musical hub of Europe. Not only was Mozart graced with prodigious talent; that talent flourished through the encouragement of a doting father. Where Salieri had to struggle to realize his modest natural gifts, the *wunderkind*'s progress was naturally accelerated. Envy of genius compounded.

Jealousy and musical transformation

What of jealousy, a similarly emotion-laced vice often entwined with envy and sometimes confused with it? Is Salieri also afflicted with jealousy? Like envy, the object of jealousy is another person whose relationship to us arouses our hostility toward him. Like envy, jealousy turns on something we value and springs from some lack in ourselves. As with envy, jealousy eats away at us; life would be much more enjoyable were we free of envy or jealousy. This much might well explain why jealousy may be confused with envy, so much do they have in common. Yet the two toxic emotional vices are different. Envy is about possessing something we desire but are without. Jealousy is about fear of losing something we possess or believe we possess. I am envious of Sam's good looks, charm, or wealth: a two-term relationship (three if we add Sam's desirable attribute). But I am jealous of Sue's (possible) affection for Sam, something I now enjoy or believe I enjoy: a three-term relationship (four if we add Sue's affection). Envy and jealousy can be entwined in the following way: I envy Sam his good looks, charm, or wealth because one (or all) of these appears to be the reason I may lose Sue's affection. The fulcrum upon which I may be deprived of the thing I value becomes, for that very reason, the object of my envy. Were it not for fear that Sam might lure Sue away from me I would not envy him his desirable attributes. Of course, jealousy need not beget envy; we might simply be jealous, afraid of losing Sue's affections, without homing in on some attribute of the person who does or might pose a threat to our well-being.

So, is there reason to think that Salieri is jealous of Mozart? Yes, but it is secondary in importance to his envy as well as secondary in the sense of derivative from his envy. As I mentioned, Salieri does rue Mozart's increasing posthumous celebrity even as his own wanes. It is fair to say then that Salieri is jealous of Mozart's fame. He did once take pride in the popularity of his own music and the accolades it brought him, telling the priest that he had been "the most popular composer in Europe." In a sense, the living Salieri has lost his fame and good repute to the deceased Mozart. As evidence of the disparity in their enduring popularity, we see that the priest is ignorant of a few tunes of his own that Salieri plays for him, but quickly and eagerly identifies Mozart's catchy and charming *Eine kleine Nachtmusik*. Salieri tells the priest that he is becoming obsolete in his own lifetime, "my music growing fainter, all the time fainter." But the jealousy is complicated by the fact that Salieri knows with certainty that Mozart's music is indeed clearly superior to his own. We might say that Salieri's jealousy is shallow, a shadow cast by the cause of the predominant envy: Mozart's musical genius.

Trying to persuade the emperor to allow him to mount a production of the *Marriage of Figaro* (which the emperor thinks might be politically dangerous), Mozart explains how he will end the second act. He excitedly asks the emperor to guess how long he can sustain the particular episode of pure song. When the bemused monarch gives up, Mozart tells him that he will begin with a duet and expand it into a trio, thence into a quartet, a quintet, a sextet, and on and on, for twenty continuous, harmonious minutes of blossoming voice. One of the court's musical officials notes that opera should be ennobling. But Mozart, the iconoclast, is tired of homages to classical heroes, blurting out that dead legends like Hercules are boring, "so lofty they sound as if they shit marble." Instead, Mozart sees opera as the opportunity to delight in exuberance, to celebrate creative play on a grand scale. Earlier, when conducting his opera *The Abduction of the Seraglio*, he could barely contain the joy he took in his own creation. With both arms above his head, elbows cocked at a ninety-degree angle, Mozart ebulliently rocks his arms left and right, as if joining the swirling, twirling dancers on the opera stage. He never stops smiling. Another example of his playfulness is soon epitomized by the delightful "pa-pa-pa-pa" sequence during the Papageno duet in *The Magic Flute*. We are reminded of the many ways in which Mozart also took lighthearted amusement in his daily life: from teasing his girlfriend or making up word games to playing Bach while held upside down at the masque party.

Disheartened by news of his father's death in Salzburg, Mozart finds inspiration in him as he undertakes *Don Giovanni*. Salieri immediately discerns and marvels at Mozart's ability to use his own life to make his art. The rival finds it "terrifying and wonderful to watch" Mozart draw upon his father's strong personality and severe presence in constructing the thunderous climax to the opera and Don Giovanni's life. The defiant roué is damned by an implacable stand-in for Leopold. Mozart will later perform a similar bit of alchemy when he transmutes his nagging mother-in-law's pecking away at him into the precious metal of the Queen of the Night's aria in his dazzling fantasy *The Magic Flute*. Playing to a crowd of common folk in a burlesque house, the impoverished composer finally receives the unqualified love (and half the gate) that had eluded him in the more refined precincts of Vienna.

Salieri assists: creation and destruction

The relative abilities of Salieri and Mozart also point to another telling feature of envy: to feel malignant envy instead of the admiration or emulative sort, the valued object must be more or less close to within our reach. This is to say that typically we envy those who are not drastically above us with regard to the thing we cherish. This condition is something like object proximity, reflecting the psychological need for a plausible explanation by which the desirable thing could have been ours. Aristotle makes the observation that envy is often felt toward people who are "like" and "equal" to us (1991: 155; 1386b). In such cases, the advantage had by the other person in comparison to ourselves is more palpable and searing since we are so otherwise similar. A merely competent bench scientist is not likely to feel vicious envy toward a world-famous scientist who wins the Nobel Prize in chemistry. The invidious comparison upon which envy is based would require such a distorted view of actual merit as to be untenable.

Hume explains the consequences of strong disparity (and corresponding lack of proximity) this way: "the great disproportion cuts off the relation, and either keeps us from comparing ourselves with what is remote from us, or diminishes the effects of the comparison" (1896: 378–79). However, another, more renowned chemist who might plausibly have been in the running for the honor could feel the vicious kind of envy. For the first scientist, the achievements of the Nobel Laureate so far eclipse his own that his imagination cannot envision it in his grasp and so does not feel slighted by the award going to her. He has not been "passed by" because he was never in the running.[2] He is more likely to feel admiration envy or be spurred to working harder by emulating the famous chemist's example.

Iago is more like the chemist who could have been a reasonable candidate for the high honor. After all his years of service to Othello, Iago does in fact believe that he has been passed over for promotion to lieutenant in favor of the younger, handsomer Cassio (the play never enlightens us as to why Othello has chosen Cassio). And this would seem true as well for Salieri. He is more than merely humdrum, having attained the highest status in the court at the musical heart of Europe. Thus it rankles that although an accomplished composer, he is clearly a cut or two below the brilliance of Mozart. It is only because he is proximate to what he cherishes that Salieri can feel rancor for someone who does enjoy it. He is good enough to imagine himself the recipient of that much more musical ability. Envy then requires proximity in status combined with disparity in our relative fortunes. We must be close enough for comparison to be plausible but distant enough to feel aggrieved by the comparison.

As he conducts or plays the keyboard during the bravura performance of *The Magic Flute*, Mozart wobbles, wavers, and finally collapses. Salieri swoops in and oversees the removal of Mozart to his home where he puts the sickly maestro to bed. Mozart thanks Salieri for coming to the performance which he pooh-poohs as mere "vaudeville." But Salieri tells him it is sublime and commends him as the greatest composer he knows. Mozart's friend, the frequent burlesque performer who had persuaded him to write for this motley crowd of theatre-goers, comes by to give Mozart his (sizable) share of the house receipts. Salieri keeps him and others of the troupe at bay, at the door, explaining Mozart's exhaustion. He then presents Mozart with the money as if it came from the mysterious stranger, the disguised Salieri, who had originally commissioned the *Requiem* from Mozart.

In a previous scene, Salieri had approached Mozart in a black cloak and mask resembling those worn by Mozart's father at the masque ball. Salieri thereby aimed to link writing the mass with the revered, deceased father to lure Mozart into a creative labor that would completely drain what waning vitality remained to him. He now tells the rumpled, clammy Mozart that the anonymous patron has promised yet another heap of coin, 100 ducats, if he can complete the masterpiece by the next night. The prospect of solvency convinces Mozart to accept Salieri's help with the work. We surmise that Salieri offers his services in finishing the *Requiem* in part to have a hand in something bound to be wonderful, though his main aim is to hasten Mozart's demise.

Here Salieri bears out Taylor's observation that envy is destructive: "Destructive thoughts and desires are a feature of the central case of [vicious] envy" (1988: 241). Most obviously, we wish the person whom we envy harm. We may actually seek to destroy the very thing that we despise the other person for possessing, even if its destruction would not give the prize to us or might cost us something else that we value. My efforts to strip the newly appointed head of my company of his position will not thereby elevate me and could result in me losing my job due to the company's declining market share. We do not gain the good by destroying it, but because the envied person no longer has the looks, wealth, or position we crave, we will no longer suffer by comparison (even if only in our own eyes). Kant analyzes the psychology of people like Salieri in this way: "To be envious is to desire the failure and unhappiness of another not for the purpose of advancing our own success and happiness but because we might then ourselves be perfect and happy as we are" (1963: 217). Speeding Mozart on his way to the grave will not miraculously transfer his genius to Salieri, but at least Salieri will not have to endure a further steady stream of incomparable music from him.

In smaller ways, Salieri had also sought to diminish Mozart's impact if not actually destroy his person. Salieri confesses to scheming to limit *Don Giovanni* to a scant five performances, thereby constraining the scope of Mozart's art and temporarily "destroying" the opera as an available, living work of art. And yet, Salieri also admits to secretly attending every performance, so wonderful was the opera. The shot of Salieri soaking up the opera presents a man at once in awe of what he is experiencing but thoroughly dismayed by it. Humbled by the sheer magnitude of musical effects Mozart has wrought, Salieri's enmity is forged; as he tells the priest, Mozart is "unstoppable." Sabotaging the very thing he truly adores, Salieri actually deprives himself of still greater joy. But no matter, undermining Mozart's career is a higher priority.

Sometimes the destruction of the desirable thing is not literal. We can figuratively destroy it, for example, by belittling it. By reframing the valuable object as not so prizeworthy after all, we can weaken our desire for it. We focus on the flaws of our neighbor's wife; we write off our colleague's promotion as entailing too much mind-numbing, pedestrian labor; we construe the honor we were denied as merely the product of cronyism. When we spoil the thing we desire by minimizing its actual worth, we must deceive ourselves. In a form of sour grapes, we convince ourselves that the object we had longed for does not possess much genuine value. To his credit, Salieri never even entertains this mode of destructiveness. At least in his retelling, Salieri is fully appreciative of Mozart's compositions and the enormous talent that produces them. Consequently, he sets about to exacerbate Mozart's already debilitated state. In the process, Salieri becomes the dying man's willing assistant.

With Salieri writing at a small desk, Mozart dictates the *Requiem* from what is to be his death bed. Sallow and hollow-eyed, Mozart feverishly, fervently barks out notes and chords with their tempo, key, instrumentation, and vocal accompaniment. Admitted into the whirlwind of Mozart's creative flights, Salieri struggles to keep up, telling Mozart to slow down or repeat what is furiously pouring out of him. As when he had read the sheet music Stanzi had brought him earlier, Salieri hears the music he transcribes. He is clearly enthralled and energized by their collaboration while Mozart is wearing down as he runs out of time. The unlikely team work through the night, and Mozart falls into an exhausted sleep, having pleaded with Salieri for respite from their labors. The scene epitomizes the paradox of Salieri's relationship to Mozart and his music: he is thrilled to be an indispensable facilitator of Mozart's last great work of art, even as doing so destroys the extraordinary talent he loves more than anything else.

Having sensed that she has been remiss in deserting her husband, Stanzi returns home with their son to find Mozart asleep and Salieri nearby, sprawled on a chaise. When Salieri explains his presence in their home by telling Stanzi that Mozart needs him, she orders him to leave. Mozart's wife is rightly suspicious of both Salieri and the *Requiem*. Mozart comes half awake and smiles at his son who has come to the bedside and is handling the coins Salieri had passed on to the creator of *The Magic Flute*. Stanzi picks up the score of the *Requiem* and demands that Mozart stop working on it, rightly claiming that "It's making him ill." When she goes to the bed, she finds her husband has quietly slipped away. The night of composing has finished the fragile genius just as it has given birth to another soaring musical achievement. As Salieri had planned, Mozart has composed a requiem for himself.

***

The film-story provides a stunning, complex portrait of envy. It does this by indicating the various dimensions of malignant envy that inform the character of Salieri: types of envy; existential seriousness; the axis of humility-arrogance; proximity; and destructiveness. Vicious envy can be primitive or sophisticated. Salieri suffers from primitive envy to the extent that he understands God's bestowal of musical genius on Mozart as shortchanging him of the extraordinary ability. In addition, Salieri suffers from sophisticated envy because Mozart's sublime music makes his rival see himself as deficient, whereas before Mozart's arrival in Vienna Salieri thought of himself as quite good, maybe nonpareil. Salieri's envy is existentially serious in that the thing he covets concerns what is foundational to his personhood: music is all that matters to him. So his envy is neither superficial nor transient. There is also proximity between Salieri's ability and Mozart's superlative talent. Because he is an accomplished composer, Salieri can envision himself blessed with a bit more facility and so within reach of Mozart's genius.

The axis of humility-arrogance cuts both ways, being relevant to both Salieri and his nemesis. Salieri's lack of humility (ironically) with regard to virtue propels his envy by providing him with a basis for feeling wronged by Mozart's superiority. Because his moral character appears better to him than Mozart's, Salieri feels justified in resenting Mozart's stellar talent. Moreover, Mozart's own arrogance heightens the older man's moral indignation by adding another moral failing to the youth's vulgarity, immaturity, and profligacy. The film unfurls the destructive nature of envy gradually until its fatal climax. Salieri begins by undermining Mozart's position with such maneuvers as feigning to help him stage *The Marriage of Figaro* and cutting short the run of *Don Giovanni*. The court composer finishes his corrosive project by spurring Mozart on in completing the work, the *Requiem*, that saps his last bit of vitality in the crowning achievement of his illustrious career. The film's finale elegantly weds Salieri's warring attitudes toward Mozart's fabulous talent: he is simultaneously instrumental to Mozart's wonderful creation as well as his lamentable destruction.

Notes

1 Please see the discussion of prostitution, literal and artistic, in the previous chapter on integrity.
2 Of course, it is psychologically possible for someone who is grossly inferior to feel envy of the vicious sort; however, such an individual would also have to suffer from the additional flaw of being delusional with regard to either his own status in relation to the valued object or the way the world actually works.

Bibliography

Aristotle (1991). *On Rhetoric: A Theory of Civic Discourse*, Trans. George Kennedy. Oxford: Oxford University Press.

Bernard of Clairvaux (1985). *The Twelve Steps of Humility and Pride and On Loving God*, Ed. and Trans. Halcyon C. Backhouse. London: Hodder and Stoughton.

Hume, David (1896). *A Treatise of Human Nature*, Bk. II, Part II, Sect. 8, L.A. Selby-Bigge. Oxford: Clarendon Press.

Kant, Immanuel (1963). *Lectures on Ethics*, Trans. Louis Infield. Indianapolis, IN: Hackett Publishing.

Rawls, John (1999). "The Problem of Envy" (from *A Theory of Justice*), *Virtuous Persons, Vicious Deeds*, Ed. Alexander Hooke, 306–11. Mountain View, CA: Mayfield Publishing.

Shakespeare, William (1954). *The Tragedies of Shakespeare*, Vol. II, Ed. Bennett Cerf et al. New York: Random House.
Snow, Nancy (1995). "Humility." *The Journal of Value Inquiry*, 29, 203–16.
Taylor, Gabriel (1988). "Envy and Jealousy: Emotions and Vices." *Midwest Studies in Philosophy*, XIII, 233–49.

Filmography

Forman, Milos (1984). *Amadeus*, U.S.

5 The virtues of aspiration
Three boys make good

Passion, self-discovery, and virtue

Three films illuminate the joys and struggles involved in young people aspiring to do what they love. The films that came out within a few years of each other, at the close of the twentieth century, are about boys who dedicate themselves to a serious lifetime discipline after discovering an affinity for it. Each film-story explores pivotal themes: passion for a particular, demanding activity; the place of imagination and aesthetic experience in this passion; and parental relationships. Flowing through these stories, connecting the thematic dimensions, are the moral virtues the boys must develop in order to realize their quest for proficiency, if not mastery, in their chosen fields. The films repay comparison because different aspects of the virtues and their interconnectedness emerge as a result of the films' overlapping themes and story lines. If the stories follow a fairly predictable arc that is because they are tales of success. To be interesting, such tales require that their protagonists face formidable challenges which, with help, they eventually overcome. Investigating this cluster of films with their handful of virtues will make this our most expansive chapter.

In each film-story, a boy is captivated by an activity that he finds inherently interesting and rewarding, worth pursuing as an end in itself, for its own sake. The stories involve a range of pursuits. Science, dance, and chess are the fields that call to the boys in *October Sky* (Joe Johnston, 1999), *Billy Elliot* (Stephen Daldry, 2000), and *Searching for Bobby Fischer* (Steven Zaillian, 1997), respectively. The boys find the purpose and objective structure of the discipline immediately worthwhile, without fully understanding it or themselves. Participating in the activities that make up the discipline presents itself to them as something of an existential imperative: their very nature demands that they engage in the relevant activities. The stories then are tales of self-discovery through a pursuit that the hero cannot resist. The pursuit will naturally entail cultivating the relevant talents that the boys possess; but in order for these diverse talents to flourish, the novices will have to develop and exercise pivotal moral virtues.

The virtues will primarily be executive in nature, strengths of character that enable us to act in ways that achieve our ends, rather than substantive virtues. The substantive virtues provide motives, such as generosity in which we give something of value for another's benefit, or justice, in which we aim for a social distribution of benefits or burdens that treats people as they deserve. But in these film-stories, the boys have found their ends – accomplishing the tasks inherent in rocketry, dance, and chess; therefore, the virtues called for are those that facilitate sustained effort and overcoming obstacles.

First, and most obviously, the boys must have perseverance. Science, dance, and chess are difficult and demand extensive, arduous work. It will take sustained effort to soldier on in these endeavors to even become competent, let alone excellent. Perseverance is the ability to screw oneself to the task, repeatedly, even when it does not go well. The hurdles the boys face are both external (in the world) and psychological (aspects of their inner lives). External impediments include socio-economic barriers and unreceptive fathers. Subjective stumbling blocks include self-doubt and the seemingly endless prospect of the grind of laborious, often repetitious, effort. The films show how perseverance depends upon a tripod of companion virtues: patience, humility, and resilience.

The demands and difficulties that make patience a virtue involve the place of time in our lives: having to wait the appropriate amount of time for events to occur or taking the time needed to perform tasks and to solve problems. Of the two extremes that are the vices pertinent to patience, impatience is the more familiar and common. It is the inability to wait or work as the necessary time passes without agitation, anxiety, or outright anger. For the opposite vice, "over-waiting" or dawdling, we have to strain to find a name. People who suffer from this vice do not act when they should or act in too desultory a manner. In our stories, the protagonists must be patient with themselves in both the performance of activities and in waiting the appropriate amount of time for their natural gifts to bear fruit; most conspicuously, taking the necessary time to learn how to do the things that go into their chosen activity, for example, to figure out the best materials for rockets, to execute a pirouette, to trap an opponent's queen. The specific, piecemeal efforts needed to acquire these abilities each takes time, and the individual who lacks patience will either fail to acquire the essential skills or acquire inferior versions of them.

But underlying this mode of patience is the other – allowing the appropriate time to pass for optimal results. Only here, the waiting involves the individual's pace in learning the relevant skills. The boys must be patient, above all, with themselves with regard to their rate of growth. And not every skill or ability that comprises a discipline advances at the same rate. The boys have to let themselves learn and grow at the pace dictated by their discipline in conjunction with their own changing levels of achievement. In all three of our film-stories, the protagonists exhibit remarkable patience with themselves, made especially noteworthy because of their youth. It is a testimony to their maturity and to the pull exerted by their aspiration.

Humility is the moral response to having a realistic estimation of ourselves. The humble person does not exaggerate the worth of his abilities (or moral character) as in arrogance, nor does he sell himself short.[1] As exhibited by Eric Liddell, in the first chapter, humility is reinforced by realizing how much our accomplishments depend on conditions beyond our control and credit. These were shown to include natural endowments, fortunate opportunities, and timely guidance. Humility is ingredient in perseverance because each boy must keep his limitations as well as his ability in the proper perspective. In each of our stories, the protagonist understands early in his quest that his own passion and talents will not be sufficient to realize that to which he aspires. Humility enables him to seek or accept the help of those more knowledgeable. Without such help, his perseverance would surely flag; we need some measure of progress to maintain the willingness and interest to keep plugging away. However, the boys must also have enough confidence in their natural ability to put in the long hours of wearing effort. Even with vital instruction and passion, there will be reversals and plateauing of skill that the youths must work through. A realistic appraisal of their strong, native potential gives them the confidence to stay the course. Otherwise, the boys would not be willing to travel on so long and steep a road that they soon see lies before them.

As we should expect of such film-stories, the boys also have to contend with setbacks and discouraging situations. To regain their zest for their essential endeavors, then, they will have to be resilient, to rebound from failure or adversity in order to continue to persevere. The resilient individual copes with daunting obstacles or setbacks, figures out ways to adapt, and continues applying himself to the tasks that then progressively emerge. Often, the individual will have to envision new possibilities or approaches in order to recover his zeal for the enterprise. Resilience is an alternative to either flat out giving up or distracting oneself through such diversions as entertainments, transient pleasures, or more facile activities. Each boy exhibits resilience in a different way, consistent with his personality, in response to his particular circumstances and family relations.

Here I want to suggest something that may at first seem counter-intuitive, viz. that aspiration itself is a moral or quasi-moral virtue. The non-moral aspect of aspiration lies in the end itself, such as perfecting one's ability to run, teach, or compose music (goals that are central in our earlier chapters). Becoming adept at a technical skill or set of skills is not in itself a moral achievement. However, moral value accompanies this technical endeavor and achievement. Submitting oneself to the discipline, becoming a disciple of dance or science, for example, has the moral value of seeking to promote an objectively worthwhile end. The individual is in effect saying that he is committing himself to a pursuit that is good apart from himself. When motivated by aspiration, the individual elevates himself by virtue of identifying with and working toward a lofty goal. The notion of self-perfection leads into the more definite concept of moral duty. As we saw in the investigation of integrity in Chapter Three, talent development itself can be construed as an imperfect moral duty. Following Kant, we can argue that although the boys do not themselves perceive it as such, they are discharging a moral duty to themselves when they improve upon their natural gifts.

As I am understanding it, aspiration resembles and overlaps with ambition. Both involve aiming to attain something higher, above what the individual presently is or has. Both involve making a determined effort over time. However, ambition need not be housed in a determinate discipline such as science, art, or sport. People can simply be ambitious for money, power, status, or promotion. As such, ambitious people need not care especially about the means used to achieve their goal; it is about acquisition or attainment, *per se*, accumulating more or rising higher. However, aspiration is a seeking after proficiency or excellence in a structured domain whose telos is measured by a standard that informs the domain. We might then think of aspiration as defined, structured ambition: ambition structured by a determinate, objectively valuable purpose requiring cultivation of a set of prescribed skills. In my view, then, ambition by itself, "raw" ambition, would not have the moral value found in aspiration.

The film-stories also indicate how inspiration can inform and motivate aspiration. For all three of our protagonists, the discipline and its constitutive activities possess an aesthetic allure. Each boy's imagination is captured by the beauty of the art, science, or game. It pulls him into its orbit, like a psychological force. Most pronounced are the aesthetic contours of their respective disciplines. The exhilaration of moving gracefully and vigorously obviously animates the dancer. The fabulous parabola of the rocket forcefully defying gravity as it soars into the sky is aesthetically thrilling. Chess is replete with aesthetic dimensions: the piercing combination of pieces on offense; the elegance of a line of play; the opening up of hitherto unforeseen possibilities on the board as the game unspools. But besides the aesthetic dimensions that reside in what we might consider the discipline's events or episodes, such as firing a rocket or launching a dance routine, the perspective on the whole enterprise is aesthetically saturated. At some point, each boy envisions himself in the extended scenario of his aspiration: trying out various options, improving his abilities, performing at ever higher levels. The boy must imaginatively project himself into a desirable future, in which his talents develop more and more fully as he becomes more accomplished.

October Sky is about a teenager in a West Virginia coal mining town who becomes enchanted with the idea of space travel and building a rocket. With no experience or understanding of what will be involved or required of him, Homer Hickam is bedazzled by the sight of Sputnik hurtling through the starry night in 1957. Entranced by the image, Homer's own imagination is fired and he is inspired to take part in the incipient venture into space. It may be the most complex of the three undertakings I examine, as it involves Homer in a multifaceted process of thinking, making, doing, observing, and revising. Homer's aspiration originates externally, from the spectacle of the Russian satellite. In the course of pursuing his passion for rocketry he will have to overcome serious obstacles, including learning a good deal of math and science, mostly on his own. The film illustrates how aspiring to a wondrous goal can motivate us to do arduous work that otherwise holds no interest at all.

In contrast to Homer being ignited by a spectacle outside himself, Billy Elliot's drive to dance comes from within. Also hemmed in by a mining town, in England, Billy simply feels the need to move rhythmically and takes unmitigated joy in the aesthetics of his bodily motion, his own kinesthetic creation. Dance is akin to the more manly artistry of boxing that he forsakes, in that it involves moving arms, legs, and torso rhythmically, with grace, in various combinations, on the ground and through the air. Although Billy may be interested in creating beauty, he is most powerfully and immediately motivated chiefly by the delight found in moving his body energetically and expressively. As with Homer in *October Sky*, Billy experiences his interest as a compulsion, as something about which he really has no choice. Dance will necessarily provide self-fulfillment, but Billy does not, or cannot, articulate that aspect of his engagement. It is just a fact about him that is inherent in his passion for the artistic activity. It is fair to say that Billy possesses an imagination that resonates to the contours of dance – a terpsichore imaginative.

In *Searching for Bobby Fischer*, Josh Waitzkin simultaneously discovers his interest in chess and his gift for the game. His motivation to play the game is a combination of the external enchantment of Homer and the inner awakening of Billy. Josh first simply enjoys watching chess played at his neighborhood Washington Square park in New York City, but soon realizes that he has exceptional ability. Josh does not seem as driven as the other two boys, yet is motivated enough to practice extensively and take (sometimes harsh) instruction in strategy and preparation. Then, too, Josh is the youngest of our trio and chess is after all a game, however complex and raised to a vocation for some practitioners. The aesthetic dimension involves imagining possible ways a given game can unfold, the beauty of competing strategies, and the artistry of adapting to one's opponent's decisions: improvising and foreseeing new possibilities within the changing configurations of the pieces on the board. *October Sky* and *Searching for Bobby Fischer* are based on actual boys and their exploits, but *Billy Elliot* has the feel of a real-life drama.

The films provide insight into a particular mode of flourishing: feeling elevated, sometimes literally lifted off the ground, by virtue of doing something found to be worthwhile for its own sake. I should qualify this claim by adding that the individual wishes to perform the activity well. Homer wants to launch rockets that go miles into the sky; Billy wants to dance expressively; and Josh wants to play skillful chess competitively. But doing the activities well are not independent ends; rather, they are the outcome of cultivating one's natural abilities in the course of engaging in the pursuit. These good are what John Kekes considers "internal" goods, "They are self-developed... they come to a person ... as a result of his inner life... The satisfaction is part of having done well" (1983: 506–07). But the goods are also "internal" to the discipline itself – the valuable qualities that are intrinsic to performing the activities constitutive of the discipline. The boys are not in it for extrinsic goods, such as the status, power, or wealth found in simple ambition. Instead, they are sustained by the satisfactions inseparable from fabricating sleek, airborne rockets; leaping and swirling in space; crafting a sequence of chess moves that exploit an opponent's vulnerability.

A word about chess. Since it is structurally competitive, to play is to match wits with an adversary and to play well will sometimes culminate in victory, which result can approach the value of an external good. For some enthusiasts, winning games or piling up championships is the reason to play, taking on an importance that eclipses the enjoyment of playing the game (as had appeared true of what motivated Abrahams to run in the first chapter). But watching Josh, we do not get the sense that he simply wants to win. A well-fought game that he lost would no doubt satisfy him more than a lopsided victory. After all, the quality of one person's play depends on the skill of his or her opponent. An accomplished opponent will push a chess practitioner to be more inventive, more resourceful, and that will yield a more invigorating match. So it is not victory as such that someone like Josh seeks, but engrossing matches that test and promote his own propensity for the game.

In the opening scenes of the film *Camille Claudel* (Bruno Nuytten, 1988), the phrase "the madness of the mud," referring to clay, crystallizes the young artist's fervor for sculpting: making, forming, almost bathing in her medium. Of course, Camille wants her work to be admired, but the madness, the need that cannot be denied is to be fabricating art with her own hands. Running is similarly essential for Liddell and Abrams, just as Salieri and Mozart need to compose music to fulfill their natures. Similarly, we might call the endeavors of the three boys "essential pursuits." First, the endeavors speak to the essence of each boy, his natural affinity, and predilection for the field. Second, the pursuit is essential to the boy's well-being. He cannot flourish unless fully engaged in the activity. When taking part in the essential pursuit, which typically also includes thinking and talking about it, the individual is most acutely alive, feels most completely one with himself. He is completely absorbed and fulfilled.

Much of the pleasure of the films comes from seeing the boys take unmitigated joy in their endeavors and come to realize that pursuing them is exactly what they must do. We see that their joy entails an enlarging appreciation. The appreciation is comprised of understanding and valuing: understanding and valuing rocketry, dance, and chess, but also understanding and valuing their own aptitude for and involvement with it. The passion is to enter into another world, defined by the relevant activity, replete with its own challenges and beauty, progress and rewards. In penetrating the mysteries and intricacies of these domains, the boys are in turn penetrated by them and transformed, ironically discovering wonderful things about themselves even as they are lifted out of themselves by the activities.

In all three film-stories, parents play pivotal roles. In the first two, working-class, mining fathers simply do not appreciate what their sons aspire to; rockets and dance seem frivolous, especially to men who labor long and hard in dangerous work to support their families. Consequently, a major obstacle that Homer and Billy must overcome is gaining their fathers' understanding of their gifts and respect for the legitimacy of their pursuits. Josh suffers from the opposite problem. His father is so gung ho about Josh's chess playing that he loses sight of the fact that his son is still a boy, and taking part in the jazz-like version of street chess may be compatible with his formal, more classical study of the game. Josh's story directly raises the question of how parents should nurture the talents of their precocious children, where nurture includes allowing (even encouraging) their offspring to be playful boys or girls. Consequently, larger lessons are implied for parents of the math prodigy, young athlete, or child musical virtuoso.

Inspiration from without

Homer (Jake Gyllenhall) grows up in the West Virginia mining town of Coalwood, where the dark of the high evening sky is juxtaposed against the inky depths of the mine: one liberating, the other suffocating. Previously indifferent to the Sputnik phenomenon, once Homer witnesses its blinking orbit in the star-speckled sky, he is completely enthralled. After the gazing crowd disperses, Homer stands transfixed, exclaiming to his mother how beautiful the satellite looked streaking across the sky. The sparkle of rocket flight has Homer in its hot grip, with the science that governs it soon to follow. All the boy wants to do is build and launch rockets that can escape into space, much as he will yearn to escape the mining town. As the mine's foreman, Homer's father, John (Chris Cooper), is its natural leader. He keeps the men productive, corrects mistakes, and saves lives in the treacherous work. Homer's rejection of the work keeps father and son in conflict, especially since John cannot see the value of Homer's aspirations. While the family is eagerly discussing Homer's brother's impending football game, Homer smiles and announces, "I'm gonna build a rocket."

His aspiration is all-consuming, but blind; Homer has no idea what rocket-building will require of him. Part of the charm of the movie-story is watching Homer take the various steps needed to make and set off rockets. These include coming to grips with the math and science that rocketry demands but that Homer previously had no real interest in. The perseverance this requires is fueled by Homer's passion for the enterprise. The perseverance extends to Homer asking for help, even when it is awkward or tricky to do so. For example, he befriends the class science geek (Quentin), despite the warning of his pals that doing so is certain social death. Any concern with social norms or expectations is obliterated by Homer's overriding commitment. He will also enlist help with welding portions of the rocket from two of the mine's machine shop experts. Homer's enthusiasm overcomes the reluctance of the first mechanic to use company equipment and time for this extra-mural purpose.

Homer has enough humility to realize how much his endeavor will depend upon ongoing assistance. After all, not everyone embarked on a steep path of hard work is willing to seek help. In order to ask other people to give us a boost, we must acknowledge our deficiency publicly and have the humility to put ourselves in the other person's debt. Humility's correlate of acknowledging our weakness and need is an equally realistic awareness of our ability. Homer's confidence in his ability to grapple with the mechanical and intellectual demands of rocketry nicely complements his recognition of just how much he cannot presently do and does not yet understand. Homer will also be bolstered by the support of his teacher Miss Riley, who defends him to the school's principal and also holds out the hope of a college scholarship. Together, with a pair of his friends, Homer and Quentin soon get to work in the basement of Homer's house.

After a rocket launch goes awry near the mine, Homer's father scolds him for his involvement with the "idiot thing," and correctly surmises that the shopworker Bykovsky has pitched in with the building of Homer's rocket. Homer accuses his father of loving the mine more than his family and rebuffs his father's plans for him, saying, "I'm never goin' down there." To escape his father's wrath, Homer leads his team to a site miles away, off the property of the mining company. Ever the visionary, he christens the location "Cape Coalwood" (after Cape Canaveral and the mining town) and points out where their blockhouse, safe command post, and launch pad will be. When Bykovsky later notes that Homer doesn't give up, Homer simply states, "I can't." He has no choice; he is compelled to pursue the activity, despite almost insurmountable difficulties: lack of knowledge and equipment, skimpy resources, and the opposition of his father. All three of our protagonists have to persevere through adversities, but Homer's seem the most debilitating. The film-story indicates that without the burning inspiration, the boy's aspiration would not be strong enough to sustain the perseverance necessary for his success.

A second shopworker, Mr. Bolden, comes to the site to watch a rocket launch, suggests that the boys lengthen the rocket and use stronger steel for the nozzle washer, and soon teaches Homer how to weld. We then see a telescoping of half a dozen launches, some more successful than others, as the team experiments with different materials, rocket lengths, and propellants. Homer's sense of humor is in evidence when he ironically names the rockets "Auk," after a flightless bird. As the story proceeds, the rockets and the ignition mechanisms grow more sophisticated, producing more effective flights. At a major launch, a crowd of students and the teacher Miss Riley gather and are rewarded when a still larger rocket just keeps soaring into the sky, seemingly forever. Thrilled with the boys' accomplishments, Miss Riley brings Homer a thick technical book on rocketry to which Homer applies himself assiduously. Homer is patient with himself – willing to take the time needed to acquire the expanding technical knowledge required to move on to each successive stage of his project. The rocket boys are further encouraged by a poetically rendered description of the flight of their rockets in a laudatory newspaper article.

Yet the article alerts the state police to the experiments and they, mistakenly, arrest the team for starting a forest fire. The boys burn their blockhouse and are resigned to abandoning their work. As if things could not get worse, Homer feels compelled to work in the mine when his father is severely injured in an accident underground, during which he saved the lives of a dozen miners. In a painful irony, Homer looks up to see the Russian satellite sailing among the stars as he descends into the mine. Homer's resilience is here put to the test as he has clearly hit the low point in his space odyssey. Fortunately, he is able to rebound from the double blow to his aspirations and get back in touch with his enthusiasm for his essential endeavor. Perhaps underlying the resilience that buoys perseverance is hopefulness – a realistic belief in achieving one's goals, even when they appear relatively remote. His clear-eyed faith in himself is embodied in Homer's usually unflagging eager and energetic demeanor. Yet even here, help from another person is pivotal.

Homer is soon encouraged by a bittersweet visit with Miss Riley who is home, suffering from a fatal strain of Hodgkin's disease. She urges her student to listen to what is inside himself, adding that he is not "supposed to end up in the mines." She tells Homer that she is proud of him. In this scene, a teacher serves to encourage her student's flagging resilience. In other films, the teacher of the aspiring boy provides technical instruction, helping Billy execute his dance movements and Josh play stronger chess. But here, Miss Riley's dying gift is a morale boost, reaffirming Homer's ability to reach into the sky and not sink down into the coal pits. The young scientist returns to his rocket text, figures out a complex equation, and establishes that the team's rocket could not, in fact, have caused the fires it was alleged to have done. His calculations are corroborated when he and Quentin locate the missing rocket in a stream, nowhere near the area of the conflagration. The boys are soon exonerated and they prepare for the state science fair.

Homer has a final showdown with his father. John tells Homer that he is proud of the work his son has been doing in the mine and that he could eventually have his leadership job. He says that Homer can keep the rocketry as a hobby but that he should not miss work, something of which he has recently been guilty. Frustrating his father still further, Homer rejects the idea of returning to the mine, "The coal mine's your life. It isn't mine. I'm never going down there again." He adds, "I wanna go into space." Moreover, Homer rightly understands that the mine and the town with it are dying.

When the boys win the state fair, Homer is the obvious choice to represent them at the national science competition in Indianapolis. We see him standing in front of the team's display and explaining it expertly, but in the night the exhibit is stolen and all seems lost, again. Although the various setbacks could easily seem excessive or contrived, the fact that the film is based on actual events injects credibility into an otherwise melodramatic tale. Problems with the state police, the father's injury, and now the theft of the project pile up, but they are part of a genuine triumphal trajectory. To add to the drama, only Homer's father can save the day. The miners have been out on strike, but if John resolves the dispute, Mr. Bolden can return to the machine shop and whip up some new display materials in time for Homer's ongoing stint at the national fair. Homer's mother tells John that if he does not come through she will leave him, tainting to some extent his good deed with the specter of coercion. But he settles the strike for Homer, who, of course, goes on to win the science fair and secure college scholarships for the whole crew! Homer's father shows up for the last launch on a bright, sunny day, in front of the whole town. John accepts the honor of igniting the rocket, named "Miss Riley," and puts his arm around his son. He finally gets it.

Aspiration is aiming for something presently out of reach, beyond one's current situation or condition. The image of the rocket taking off and climbing into the clouds is almost too apt for my purposes, so perfectly does it emblematize aspiration. But it also makes *October Sky* the ideal film with which to launch this examination of the web of virtues woven through the stories of the boys who feel compelled to heed the call of an activity that so clearly speaks to them.

Expression from within

Where Homer is inspired by an external image, a fabulous starry spectacle, Billy Elliot harkens almost exclusively to an internal force that is pushing to express itself, through his body, in the world. Although he has to be exposed to the formal positions of ballet, he is attracted to the art because dance is in his blood. The opening scene is of Billy in a tank top and shorts, leaping to music: turning in air, throwing up his arms, spinning, running above his bouncy bed. Billy feels the music, whose lyrics include "Danced myself right out the womb" (*Cosmic Dancer*, T. Rex); moving his body is that primal an urge for the boy. As with Homer's lack of football talent, Billy is not cut out for the manly sport of boxing. However, due to the soup kitchen set up to serve the striking miners, Mrs. Wilkerson's ballet class now occupies a portion of the boxing hall where Billy is supposed to train. Billy is drawn to the all-girls class as if by a magnet. Much of Billy's story mirrors Homer's: unreceptive fathers, more typical macho brothers, supportive teachers, and undeniable thirst for something alien to their mining towns.

Billy soon joins the ballet class on the sly, loaned a pair of dance slippers by the teacher, and encouraged by her daughter. The precocious Debbie tries to assuage Billy's gendered trepidations by assuring him that lots of men perform ballet and are not "poofs" but excellent athletes. As with Homer, Billy reads up on his pursuit, practicing the basic positions at home as well as during Mrs. Wilkerson's lessons. He is awkward, but persistent. Billy perseveres despite his incipient physical limitations and the social stigma of engaging in a girlish art form in a starkly masculine milieu because the feeling he gets when he dances is undeniably electrifying and inspiring. He is not yet aspiring to some apprehended level of mastery, but under the teacher's blunt tutelage, Billy finally manages a successful spin without falling.

Billy perseveres in pursuit of his passion, but unlike Homer, Billy is not yet self-conscious about where he wants to go with it or where it might take him. We see Billy running and dancing down the street with total abandon. We can practically feel his aesthetic experience: the constant stream of rhythmic vitality in his nerves and muscles, the literal fibers of his being. Dance courses through him like a current; he is more a conduit of an energy already in motion than its initiator. As his gay friend will later call him, Billy is indeed a "dancing boy," much as Aristotle refers to certain gifted people as "musical men." Billy is beginning to sense how his primitive impulse might take shape, how it might become a genuine focused and long-term pursuit. And that pursuit is one that will require patience, as in doggedly repeating the maneuver until he can spin without flopping, and a healthy dollop of humility. The young man quickly understands that he cannot simply freelance, but will need a great deal of instruction.

As with Homer's fraught paternal encounter, Billy must contend with his father's displeasure when the striking miner finds Billy in the ballet class instead of sparring in a boxing ring.[2] When his father splutters that "lads do football or boxin' or wrestling," Billy quotes Debbie on ballet dancers being fit as athletes and not gay. Neither father can appreciate the son's passion nor see the activity from his point of view. Just like Homer, Billy finds a way to continue with his essential endeavor; he works privately with Mrs. Wilkerson, who tells him that she thinks he has a chance at the prestigious Royal Ballet School in London. When Billy protests his lack of training, the teacher tells him the school can teach him that, prophetically adding, "It's how you move and how you express yourself that's important."

One special session with Mrs. Wilkerson begins with Billy sharing a letter his late mother had written to him when her death was imminent, and culminates in a rousing duet. Besides talking about how much Billy means to her, his mother writes that he should "always be yourself," echoing Miss Riley's dying advice to Homer. Following his teacher's instructions, Billy has brought some items to suggest ideas for dance, including a soccer ball and some music.[3] He and Mrs. Wilkerson do a spirited (apparently improvised) number to "I Love to Boogie," incorporating tap, modern dance, and ballet. But friction at home, where both Billy's father and brother are miners struggling through their long strike, causes Billy to lash out at his mentor. He accuses her of wanting his audition for the special school for her own sake. When she, in turn, berates him for not practicing or concentrating, he exclaims, "Don't pick on me because you fucked up your own life." They reconcile, and Billy resumes practicing. But the social tensions in the town, coupled with the transgressiveness of Billy's particular art form in his socio-economic circumstances, are serious hurdles for an aspiring male dancer.

Riding on a ferry, Mrs. Wilkerson tells her star student the story of the ballet "Swan Lake." For a few hours every night a young woman, otherwise a swan, can be her human self. Billy too is constrained, almost disguised, by the hardscrabble environs that inhibit him from realizing his true nature except when free to dance. Although we do not discover where exactly the boat is taking them, the ferry symbolizes a transition between two worlds. Billy's transition will be from the numbing confines of a mining district to the liberating world of professional dance. But first, he must navigate the shoals and undertow of home and town, and then be impressive enough at his audition to vault into a promising future.

As a result of more strike conflict with the police, Billy watches as his brother is beaten and carted away. He skips the audition Mrs. Wilkerson had planned in order to attend his brother's hearing or arraignment. When she goes to Billy's home, there is a showdown over Billy's talent and future. The brother is pugnacious and scoffs at the notion that Billy could be a ballet dancer and his teacher fights back. Billy flees the escalating altercation and transforms his frustration into creative expression. The transformation can be seen as a mode of resilient adaptation; rather than giving up or venting in a direct way, Billy uses the very pursuit under siege as a way of coping and persisting. Beginning with tap dance near the family's outhouse, he bounces off tenement walls, grabs railings, dances up and down steps – employing his physical surroundings much as Fred Astaire routinely did in his films. Billy taps away, spinning, leaping, and kicking down the street: forward, backward, and sideways, finally ending at a rusting, corrugated fence – a grim reminder of the gritty world he inhabits.

Billy brings his gay friend to the gym hall and adorns the closeted cross-dresser, fittingly, in a tutu. Walking home at night, Billy's father sees light and hears music wafting from the hall. He enters and stands still. Billy commences an informal, familial audition by standing defiantly before his father. Stomping, tapping, twirling, leaping, and spinning, Billy moves with energy and grace, smoothly and brusquely. He finishes with a powerful series of swirling spins, coming to rest in front of his father. His father walks away without a word. He answers our wonder as to whether he has understood his son's talent by running to the teacher's home and asking, "How much is it gonna cost?" He even enrolls as a strike-breaking scab to raise the necessary money for the audition. When older son Tony holds him back, Frank sobs, "He may be a fuckin' genius for all we know," and tells the boy that they need "to give Billy a chance." Pawning his late wife's jewelry seems to solve the problem of funds for the prestigious audition. The mother's supporting letter is thereby figuratively embodied in the money she indirectly, posthumously provides her gifted son.

Billy's father, not his teacher, takes him to the grand estate in Newcastle for the tryout. Billy performs an interpretive number to folk music and the judges look a bit taken aback, presumably because he does not give them classical ballet. As he pirouettes and gestures with his arms, the panel look interested but somewhat bemused. Their lack of obvious enthusiasm throws Billy. When he returns with his father to the panel of judges after changing back into street clothes, he responds "I don't know," to the question of why he first became interested in ballet. They are about to leave when another judge fortuitously asks, "What does it feel like when you're dancing?"

Billy's self-reflection is a revelation. He starts off tentatively: "Don't know. Sort of feels good." He pauses, clearly considering this most vital experience for the first time. "Once I get goin' then I, like, forget everythin'. And, sort of disappear." He pushes on, "Sort of disappear. Like I feel a change in me whole body. Like there's a fire in me body. I'm just there, flyin'... like a bird. Like electricity. Yeah. Like electricity." The panel reacts with subdued appreciation, maybe a little awe. Although Billy's natural medium for self-expression is his body in motion, he has managed to give voice, however haltingly, to the aesthetic transport dance is for him.

Of course, it is plainly fitting that in our most artful of the boys' pursuits, the inspiration that bursts into aspiration is aesthetically charged experience. There can be no doubt, for the judges or us, that Billy is the genuine article: a person for whom only this art can enable him to so be himself that he is lifted out of himself, consumed as if on fire or electrified. Billy's behavior and his description of how he feels may put us in mind of the ecstasy Liddell expresses in his body and face when he runs. As his running builds momentum, Liddel's arms flail, his chest lifts, and his head tilts heavenward, transfigured. Dance is for Billy an essential endeavor and the panel knows it. Of course, Billy gets into the Royal Ballet School and we see him, grown up, leaping gracefully in what appears to be "Afternoon of the Fawn" in the film's finale.

Talent, play, and parents

Unlike our first two young protagonists, Josh Waitzkin (Max Pomeranc) is growing up in a comfortable, loving middle-class family, with no older (more rugged) brother or discouraging father. On the contrary, the enthusiasm his father (Joe Mantegna) exhibits for Josh's chess precociousness actually becomes a hurdle for his seven-year-old son to overcome. Consequently, the intensity of Fred's ardor raises a new question with regard to natural gifts: how should parents nurture their children's abilities, particularly when they are extraordinary? Fortunately for Josh, his mother Bonnie (Joan Allen) provides a needed counterpoise, insisting that Josh have fun. Implicit in her stance is giving needed weight to the fact that Josh is a child, a young one at that. Her perspective is reinforced by the personality and training of another exceptional chess boy, Jonathan, who serves as an obvious foil for Josh. Chess completely consumes Jonathan's life, resulting in a unidimensional, churlish whiz kid. The film suggests that Josh's parents, together, offer complementary aspects of the optimum approach to fostering children's natural gifts: joyfulness and play (mother) as well as seriousness and work (father).

Following Homer and Billy, Josh also receives instruction; however, his is doubled. Reflecting the divergent attitudes of his parents are the formal pedagogy of a retired chess expert Bruce Pandolfini (Ben Kingsley) and the intuitive, freewheeling advice of the park-playing, black hustler Vinnie (Laurence Fishburne). In its climactic tournament scene, the film, perhaps too obviously, indicates again that each coach contributes to the balance that makes Josh and his chess play so exceptional. Naturally, it is Vinnie and his streetwise play and pervasive trash talk that first attracts Josh to the world of chess.

As indicated, Josh's aspiration is roused by a synthesis of Homer's external inspiration by Sputnik and Billy's internal verve that begets his dance. Watching the men play pick-up chess in Washington Square Park first beguiles the pensive boy who just watches, but the experience soon awakens his natural brilliance for the game. For example, after noticing Josh play a neighboring, grumbly old Russian, Vinnie chortles that the young boy uses combinations of pieces to attack. And the more-restrained Bruce later compares Josh's vision and creativity to none less than the great Bobby Fischer, who provides the film with its overarching conceit. Throughout the movie, Josh narrates Bobby Fischer's life, chess career, and disappearance(s) as the screen offers newsreel clips of the boy wonder talking and playing. His mythic status is shown to shadow the entire chess subculture, infiltrating and perhaps animating Josh.[4] Consumed by chess, Fischer may also be functioning in the film-story the way Jonathan does, as a cautionary figure of distorted excess.

After Josh beats him in a game during which he calls out moves from the bathtub, without seeing the actual board, his father (Fred) seeks out the retired chess expert Bruce Pandolfini to be his son's teacher. Reluctant at first, Bruce agrees to take on the novice after seeing the seven-year-old play at his club and then at the park. The movie establishes Josh's sweet nature early on. First, he offers his opponent in Bruce's club his candy as a consolation prize after defeating him; next, he asks his mother whether Vinnie sleeps in the park, suggesting that the chess hustler could sleep in one of the bunk beds in his room. After the film's climactic tournament, Josh will encourage a younger chess player whom he has befriended. His kindness emerges later as a crucial ingredient during the dramatic showdown in the film's finale.

Bruce begins instructing Josh by telling him to figure out a sequence of moves, and swipes the board clear of pieces to force Josh to visualize the combinations in his head. To motivate his young pupil, he shows him a (bogus) certificate of accomplishment, indicating that Josh is earning "master chess points" toward securing the precious document. Bruce soon argues that the kind of speed chess played by such denizens of Washington Square Park as Vinnie will develop habits in Josh that will be detrimental to his growth as a competitive tournament player. Park play rewards short-term tactics over position or strategy and intimidating moves such as bringing the queen into the fray quickly. Bruce clearly favors the classical, well-planned approach over the more romantic, flamboyant, and intuitive play encouraged in the fast-paced park combat. Where Bruce emphasizes picturing a complex series of future moves, Vinnie urges Josh to play from his gut and be daring: "Always attack. Even when you retreat, you attack." Although Fred immediately agrees to Bruce's restriction, Josh's mother promptly issues a flat "No." Pointing out that Josh loves playing in the park, her son's happiness is more important to Bonnie than his progress as a chess prodigy. She breezily dismisses Bruce's complaint that allowing Josh this freedom will make his job harder. In between winning his first tournaments, we see Josh throwing a ball at Bruce's chess club, suggesting that chess is another form of play for him, however more cerebral. The trophies do pile up though.

In the park, Josh is abashed by the stellar play of another young star, Jonathan. Jonathan is overly competitive, taking delight in crushing his opponents. Instead of Josh's gentle, wide-eyed demeanor, Jonathan wears a near-sneer. We later learn that Jonathan's parents have handed him over to his teacher, an unwelcome former acquaintance of Bruce's, and that the boy does nothing but study and play chess: no regular school, no play, probably no friends. Intimidated by Jonathan, Josh expresses hesitation about participating in an imminent tournament. He is afraid of losing and looking bad. He muses to his father, "Maybe it's better not to be the best. Then, if you lose, it's O.K." The pressure of being highly ranked is onerous. To avoid later disaster at the hands of Jonathan in the tournament, Josh intentionally loses quickly, in his first match with another boy. During his postmortem, in the rain, Fred expresses his frustration with his son's play and attitude, but relents and embraces Josh when the crestfallen boy humanizes their interaction, asking, "Why are you standing so far from me?"

A telling scene between Bruce and Josh follows. Bruce asks Josh if he knows what contempt means. He tells his protégé that it means seeing others as beneath you. Josh replies, "I don't feel that way." Bruce persists, saying that thinking that other people don't belong in the same room with you is part of winning. Jonathan, for example, clearly sees victory in chess as a way to demonstrate his superiority. Here, we have arrogance extolled as if it were a virtue instead of a vice. By rejecting Bruce's praise of arrogance, Josh implicitly asserts the virtue of humility. Just as he does not see his comfortable middle-class life as making him too good to welcome Vinnie as a bunkmate, Josh does not view his chess ability as a basis for looking down on other players. Josh's ingrained humility will keep him from permitting success in one small corner of the world to enlarge his sense of overall worth. A moral maturity far ahead of his chronological age.

When Bruce says that Josh has to hate his opponents, the boy protests, "But I don't." Bruce tries invoking the legend, "Bobby Fischer held the world in contempt." Josh may be gentle, but he holds his ground with quiet strength, saying, "I'm not him." Feeling contentious when they begin to play, Josh obstinately insists on one of the special certificates that Bruce has held out as a prize. Bruce disdainfully begins tossing certificate after certificate on the table to indicate their worthlessness. Bonnie responds to this hurtful show of pique by throwing Bruce out of the house. Bonnie tells Fred, "He knows you think he's weak. But he's not weak. He's decent." The regard Josh's mother has for her son's character and happiness is an instructive corrective to overly zealous parental commitment to their offspring's talent and achievement. Ironically, the playful aspect of Josh's life and street chess games will bolster his resilience later, when Josh seems resigned to take the game more seriously, as a job, than he wishes to.

All the boys exhibit the virtues that are auxiliary to perseverance: patience, humility, and resilience. However, Josh discloses another moral aspect of an aspirational pursuit. It can jeopardize existing virtues or foster vice. The example of Josh invites us to consider an alternative scenario in which a boy like him has his sweet nature worn away, replaced by something like the callousness that defines Jonathan. After all, unbridled competitiveness must have prompted the contestant in the national science fair to filch Homer's rocket display. Josh's resistance to Bruce's caustic blandishments underscores the perils to the character of persevering long and hard, particularly in the young whose moral character is still being formed. Too easily, the rigors of demanding study and practice may encourage vices that can masquerade as strength, such as arrogance (masquerading as confidence) or contempt (wearing the guise of competitive fortitude).

Josh studies strategies and takes notes in his room, now denuded of all his childish mess, as if his childhood has been erased as well. When Fred gives him permission to quit, Josh says, "I have to win. You told me to." He continues, it "isn't just a game." Josh exhibits exceptional resilience because he perseveres despite the fact that he no longer experiences the unalloyed joy of playing the game he loves. Up until now, the hard work of studying and practicing has been tempered by the fun of playing and the excitement of learning. Fred sees the error of his ways and brings Josh to the park, which had been out of bounds, where the boy asks Vinnie, "Wanna play?" When delight replaces drudgery, perseverance comes more easily, even as a bit of success spurs us on through frustrating headwinds. During their rapid-fire game, Vinnie coaches, "You got to risk everything. You got to go to the edge of defeat… Never play the board. Always play the man."[5] Vinnie also peppers his instruction with encouragement, grunting: "Good. Yes. Better. Yeah, yeah." The game and Vinnie's palaver come to an end when Josh puts him in checkmate. They smile at one another and perform their special handshake.

Fred will shortly tell Bruce that Josh likes playing again, for the first time in a long time – because the play in the park is actually more playful – free, flowing, and exhilarating. Fred follows this up with a two-week, chess-free fishing trip as a prelude to the major, impending tournament: the competitive climax of the film. As with Homer's team winning the national science fair and Billy gaining admission to the elite ballet school, Josh will triumph over his prodigious nemesis. The arcs of the three film-stories provide the same dramatic payoff, each promising a rosy future for its blossoming protagonist. The fact that the narratives of Homer and Josh are based on the actual events that occur in the lives of real people, however, softens the clichéd feel of the "Triumphant Climax."

Vinnie has accompanied the family to the tournament and Bruce shows up in Josh's hotel room despite previously demurring. Josh tells his teacher that he cannot beat Jonathan. Bruce sympathetically replies, "You may be right. I'm not supposed to say that." Bruce is no longer worried about fostering a fighting spirit. Instead, he has come to express affection. He presents Josh with his own crafted certificate and tells him, "I've never been so proud of anyone in my life." He looks at Josh with love, and says, "I'm honored to call myself your teacher." Josh says that he is scared, comes into Bruce's arms, and they hug. His relationship with Josh has brought forth Bruce's better angels; but of course, he still wants Josh to win.

The quartet of parents and teachers watches on a closed-circuit television as Josh brings his queen into action early, following the aggressive tactics of Vinnie but flouting Bruce's more deliberate approach. The group is disheartened when Jonathan promptly gobbles up Josh's most powerful piece on the board. Whether Josh has made a mistake or has used a ploy to gain board position, as Vinnie claims, he soon evens the score by capturing Jonathan's queen through a well-placed check. Glued to the screen, Bruce urges Josh to pause and visualize the entire endgame. He quietly narrates the twelve moves ahead that will secure the victory for Josh, and shortly intuits that Josh has indeed himself pictured the sequence to success. Instead of eagerly pouncing on his opponent, however, Josh generously offers Jonathan a draw and a chance to share the championship. Jonathan rejects the offer, believing that he has the superior position and soon goes down to defeat, just as Bruce had foreseen.

Josh has taken the feel-good finales of our brace of aspiration films to another level by adding the moral virtue of generous-heartedness. Rather than being generous with material goods such as money, Josh is generous with his heart, offering something of emotional value to Jonathan. Aspiration does not override Josh's inherent kindness. Where earlier he had given his candy to the man he had beaten in Bruce's chess club and suggested to his mother that Vinnie could sleep in his room, now he holds out sharing a victory to a boy who would never himself dream of bestowing such a prize. As the film is based on a true story, we can only hope that this crowning moral action is not mere cinematic embellishment because it adds an important layer to our tales of *wunderkind* achievement. It adds the moral layer of generosity in the most competitive of the boys' enterprises, an endeavor that necessarily depends on striving to best an opponent. Yet, within this domain, Josh instinctively extends the ultimate gift, easily and naturally, without prompting.

***

The three films I discuss are about boys uncovering their hidden talents in the course of realizing a passion for their respective disciplines or practices: rocketry, dance, and chess. They all succeed in achieving a large measure of mastery of these practices because they cultivate the virtues that enable perseverance. The virtues enable the boys to persist in developing the requisite skills for their success, overcoming a variety of obstacles such as discouraging or overzealous fathers, skimpy resources, and simply the intimidating prospect of the difficulty inherent in their disciplines. We root for the boys, in part because as they embark on their quests, they are unaware of how much will be demanded of them. Then, as they grasp the extent of the work involved, we pull for them because they are exuberant in their willingness to undertake the requisite labors. In the end, the films crystallize the depths of the love of a discipline and the love of oneself that follows in general, but especially when one is actively engaged in and with rocket-building, dancing, and playing chess.

Notes

1 I am going to take the liberty of departing from customary practice by favoring male pronouns. Because it is more congruent with the film texts, doing so seems acceptable. *Akeelah and the Bee* (Doug Atchsion, 2006) is an excellent aspiration film about a black girl, with an oppositional mother rather than father. Nevertheless, comparing stories about three boys enabled me to keep a sharper focus without funneling attention into issues of race and gender, however compelling these issues are in their own right.
2 The conditions for the film-story may well have been loosely based on the lengthy, bitter miner's strike of 1984 (the year in which the film narrative is set) in the northern Yorkshire area of England.
3 Contrast this with Fletcher's lack of interest in his students' tastes and experiences. As noted in the second chapter, on arrogance, the jazz instructor is too self-absorbed to care about the musical lives of his pupils and does not spend any time instructing them on the jazz pieces they play as an ensemble.
4 Along with Josh's voice-over and the newsreels, Fischer's name is invoked intermittently within the narrative itself in almost reverential tones. The film thereby dramatizes the hold a larger than life figure has on the popular imagination, in the manner of such other legends of games as Babe Ruth.
5 This may bring to mind a similar scene from a film that came out a few years before *Searching for Bobby Fischer*. In Boaz Yakin's *Fresh* (1994), another black, park chess player exhorts his teenage son with a characterization of his own play: "I play my opponent. If he likes to attack, I force him to defend himself. If he's a cautious man, I draw him into dangerous waters." The boy, Michael, insightfully applies his father's advice beyond the chess board to the drug dealers who control the lives of himself and his addicted sister in order to free the two of them for a new life.

Bibliography

Kekes, John (1983). "Constancy and Purity." *Mind*, 92, 499–518.

Filmography

Atchison, Doug (2006). *Akeelah and the Bee*, U.S.
Daldry, Stephen (2000). *Billy Elliot*, U.K.
Johnston, Joe (1999). *October Sky*, U.S.
Nuytten, Bruno (1988). *Camille Claudel*, France.
Yakin, Boaz (1994). *Fresh*, U.S.
Zaillian, Steven (1997). *Searching for Bobby Fischer*, U.S.

6 The calamity of vanity in *Young Adult*

The force of vanity

Jason Reitman's film *Young Adult* (2011) provides a stunning portrayal of the destructive repercussions of vanity and how it is entwined with other moral vices. Mavis Gary (Charlize Theron) decides to try to rekindle the passionate relationship she once had with her high school sweetheart Buddy Slade (Patrick Wilson), which Mavis believes or hopes has been smoldering for almost two decades. What prompts Mavis's impulsive foray into the past and her hometown of Mercury, Minnesota, is discovering that Buddy has just become a father. Apparently a successful ghostwriter for a "young adult" series of formulaic novels whose market is teenage girls, Mavis's life in Minneapolis is an empty one. Her marriage has ended in divorce and she is shown to lack the fulfillment that meaningful relationship, romantic or otherwise, can provide. What could convince her to return to the small town she despises in order to woo a married, former beau? We soon realize that it is vanity coupled with the loneliness of her own childless and relation-less life. Reclaiming Buddy is supposed to fill the void in Mavis's life and confirm that she still possesses the youthful charms that bedazzled boys back in the day.

To increase the chance that her ill-conceived scheme will pan out, Mavis takes great pains to buff her already attractive image. Punctuating the film story, we see her getting a manicure, pedicure, facial, and attending assiduously to her makeup and coiffure. This alerts us to the contours of vanity, which often focuses on appearance. In analyzing vanity, A.T. Nuyen emphasizes the desire to be seen, admired, and to impress people. He cites Jos Sedley of Thackeray's *Vanity Fair* as someone who is vain with respect to his accomplishments as well as his appearance, arguing that vanity "involves extravagant behavior, either in adorning oneself in extravagant clothing or make-up, or surrounding oneself in luxury, or showing off items of social prestige such as money, status, titles, positions, and fame" (1999: 614). In short, vain individuals want to be seen, and seen as possessing something of value that others lack: "The vain person craves the attention of others, seeks to be noticed by others" (1999: 615).

Feminine vanity is often associated with women's sexuality. Here, Ann Garry follows Sandra Bartky in aligning women's vanity with their sexual appeal, at least in the popular imagination: "Perhaps the most common image of feminine vanity is that of a woman primping in front of a mirror imagining her sexual desirability to real or fantasized men" (1982: 148). The film's depiction of Mavis dwelling on her appearance certainly fits this stereotype. Garry proceeds to speculate that there might well be a difference between feminine vanity that concerns one's body in general and instances of vanity that pertain to one's "sexual being." Insofar as Mavis seeks to rekindle Buddy's attraction to her, her vanity does focus on her erotic allure. However, there are numerous places in the film that underscore Mavis being excessively proud of her writing as well as her initiative in escaping the suffocating confines of Mercury.

I would add that the corresponding attitude is essential to vanity: excessive concern with the aspect of the self that the individual prizes. Consequently, the vain individual spends an inordinate amount of time thinking about and attending to what we can consider the "object" of vanity. For Mavis, the objects of her vanity are her good looks and her authorship, probably in that order. Kant takes us more deeply into the psychology that underlies the outward manifestations of vanity. Kant views vanity as a perverse kind of ambition. Morally legitimate ambition springs from a "true love of honour,... being honoured for personal worth," whereas "To aim at gaining respect by dress, or by titles, or by any other things which are not inherent in our person, is vanity" (1963: 188). This "lust" for honor then is a perversion of the morally upright "love" of honor, just as sexual lust (for Kant) is a perverse form of genuine love for another person. Kant considers vanity, or distorted lust for honor, to be a dimension of snobbery.

Consonant with the centrality of moral law and good will in his philosophy, Kant completes his indictment of vanity by pointing out that what the snob values is trivial, certainly in comparison with the moral law and the respect we should have for it. He writes, "The snob is vain in matters of social precedence, attaches importance to things which are of little account... He aims at titles and position, and the appearance of gentility" (1963: 238). The major problem besetting the vain person then is in missing the moral boat; she mistakenly values what is of little worth and fails to properly value what is of supreme worth. Even if the object of vanity has some (non-moral) value, such as artistic or scientific achievement, the vain person pursues it for the wrong reason. She pursues the non-moral good for her own self-satisfaction and glorification instead of the goodness of the end itself.

In the course of analyzing *Young Adult*, I will revisit the two other signature vices scrutinized in this book: envy and arrogance. Although it hardly establishes a fabled unity of vice (or virtue), the discussion does explain a bit of how different vices work together or encourage one another. For example, Nuyen insightfully extends his analysis, pointing out that "vanity also contributes to other vices such as jealousy, envy, and wrath" (1999: 624). Because a vain person cares predominantly for admiration, her position relative to other individuals is uppermost in her mind. Comparison is paramount; therefore, when she perceives herself to have less of something she values, typically the object of vanity itself, she will be prone to envy those who have it to a greater degree. In such a way, vanity is a correlative of envy; both concern the self, but in relation to the valued possessions of others. We will see how the film's depiction of Mavis draws out this intimate connection between vanity and envy. She envies Buddy's wife an array of things: her domestic joy with Buddy and their baby; the good will of the town folks; and the camaraderie of her all-girl bandmates. We might say here that envy is pulled along in the frothy wake of vanity, just as Mavis's deluded thinking, insensitivity, and cruelty similarly issue from the distorting force of vanity.

Besides envy, arrogance seems a natural cousin of vanity. As Kant notes, "the arrogant demand to be noticed" (1963: 188). The overestimation of the object of vanity can be the basis for arrogance, narrowly understood in Kant's sense, or more broadly as having an "excessively high self-estimation" (1998: 383). Vanity can be a force that encourages this vice, as its companion or auxiliary, because they are kindred flaws in that both involve an excessive and harmful overestimation of self. In the case of vanity, the individual has an inflated value of an aspect of herself, such as Mavis's looks or her writing skill. Arrogance is more encompassing, proclaiming the individual's overall superiority, as we saw in Chapter Two, exemplified by Brodie and Fletcher. I should caution however that one can be vain without being arrogant, as the valuing of the object of one's vanity need not form the basis of a more generalized superiority. The inflation of self-worth can thereby remain localized, anchored to the attribute or possession about which the individual is vain. When so fenced off, then, the vain individual does not view herself as better than other people *simpliciter*, merely on the basis of shining in this one respect. The film, however, does portray Mavis's vanity as feeding arrogance. She sees herself as better than the people whom she has left behind in Mercury and boasts about it.

Mavis's arrogance manifests itself in both big and small ways. The idea that she can uproot her old boyfriend from his wife and newly arrived child is most blatantly a grand (and grandiose) exhibition of arrogance. It trumpets Mavis as so wonderful as to completely overshadow the joys and responsibilities of Buddy's life with wife and newborn, in addition to the reassuring rhythms of his familiar interactions, such as daily lunch with his father. Yet the small indications of Mavis's arrogance provide a humorous undercurrent of pizzazz to the film's picture of the ways in which her vanity colors the various details of her mundane interactions. Two bookend scenes with the clerk at the counter of the motel in Mercury where Mavis holes up are especially effective. When checking in, Mavis obviously lies about having a dog with her, even though its presence in her bag resting on the counter is evident. Then, when checking out, Mavis defiantly procures a donut from a stack that the clerk had pointedly, and officiously, told her was off limits except for "honor" guests. The disdainful superiority Mavis displays is all the more cinematically effective because it is visited so gratuitously upon someone who is, after all, Mavis's inferior.

As I analyze the film-story more directly and in detail, I will emphasize the way Mavis's vanity, often in concert with her arrogance, warps her perception of reality and disposes her to be insensitive and cruel. In these ways, then, the influence of vanity is responsible for still other flaws, both cognitive and moral. At the climax of the film, all of Mavis's defects are witnessed by a gathering of Buddy's friends and family, producing in Mavis the salutary experience of shame. It is the perfect correlate to her vanity. For where vanity motivates the individual to seek out the gaze and admiration of other people, shame is the unwelcome response to that gaze when it is disapproving. Shame is the negative mirror-image of vanity, creating a yearning for concealment instead of exposure.

The return of the native

After arriving back in Mercury, Mavis soon bumps into a former classmate in a bar. Matt Freehauf (Patton Oswalt) is obviously still under the spell of the high school beauty queen, the proverbial dork worshipping at the feet of the goddess. Mavis unabashedly tells Matt of her scheme to reclaim Buddy. It is as if the image she retains of herself as the former irresistible knockout is felt by her to be a cloak protecting her from censure. Where most people would be secretive about her morally questionable plan, Mavis is brazen, so sure is she of its rectitude and imminent success. Matt wisely cautions Mavis to keep her amorous conniving to herself and to seek professional help for her twisted understanding of her relationship with Buddy. It is fair to say that Mavis's vanity fosters a delusional perspective, on both herself and how others view her. The film does a masterful job in showing how untethered, untempered vanity, here concerning appearance, can so magnify an individual's overall self-assessment that her perception of reality becomes seriously distorted.

Buddy responds to Mavis's phone call in a friendly but not overly enthusiastic way. Her carefree come on is juxtaposed with his discharging baby care duties. Mavis's cover story for returning home is a half-baked explanation about a real estate meeting. Because Buddy puts her off for a day, instead of rendezvousing with her ex, Mavis winds up chatting with Matt in the bar. Mavis's vanity and vanity-fed arrogance make her insensitive and cruel, both of which eventually inflict more suffering on her than on others. She seems oblivious to the needs and welfare of Buddy and his family. Even a modicum of sensitivity to his well-being would have served as a check on Mavis's machinations at the outset. Later, when confronted with Buddy and his family, the reality of what she is embarking on would surely have dissuaded someone who genuinely cared about the happiness of her former love interest. Yet all such considerations get subordinated to, if not obliterated by, Mavis's self-centered plan. Her vanity completely dominates her perspective and thinking, giving shape and direction to her neediness. In the end, it begets cruelty. Had Mavis actually succeeded in reawakening Buddy's affection, she would have hurt his wife and child in the most palpable way.

At the bar, Matt clearly remembers Mavis, including details of her high school days and current life. After downing about half a dozen shots of booze, Mavis notices that Matt has a cane attached to an arm cuff. She then remembers him as "the hate crime guy," a student who was badly beaten by high school thugs for being gay. To Matt's chagrin, she keeps repeating the label, compelling him to explain that he is not gay and how the thrashing has left him permanently, physically impaired, including his sexual apparatus. A bit tipsy, Mavis confides that she is in town to reclaim Buddy Slade because they "are meant to be together." Mavis can write for a young adult audience because two decades after graduating high school she still thinks and speaks in a banal, teenage vernacular. After asking whether Mavis is joking, Matt counsels her to keep her plan to herself and to speak with a therapist. Mavis jauntily replies, with the cliché, "Love conquers all." She will later, while shopping for a dress, indiscriminately disclose her homewrecking intentions to a saleswoman, who is suitably appalled.

The next day, in preparation for getting together with Buddy, Mavis follows up a pedicure with leg-shaving, face creaming, and expert application of make-up. Dolled up in a slinky black dress, Mavis is clearly overdressed in comparison with the workmanlike attire Buddy sports. Mavis is put out to discover that Matt is also on these premises, working in this bar, different from the pub at which they met the previous night. After Buddy arrives at Mavis's table, Matt pointedly reinforces the solidity of Buddy's domestic life and Mavis glares at him. Matt takes the hint and declines Buddy's offer to join them, leaving Mavis alone with her prey. Buddy invites Mavis to his house for the next night for dinner, to be followed by a trip to a bar to hear his wife's all-girl band play.

Mavis soon calls Matt to clarify the history of her relationship with Buddy in an attempt to justify her behavior and winds up going to his house, where he has a distillery in his garage which serves as his man-cave. Matt's other hobby is working on plastic action figures of superheroes – his own arrested development. Explaining the niceties of his most special whiskey, Matt gives Mavis a high-end sample; but instead of sipping it, Mavis throws it back. They proceed to imbibe extensively and Mavis continues to drink heavily throughout her hometown sojourn. She will later suggest to her parents that she is an alcoholic, which they immediately and thoughtlessly dismiss.

Having spruced herself up, including a manicure that reprised her earlier pedicure, Mavis arrives at Buddy's home, where she meets his pretty wife Beth and their baby. She reminisces inappropriately about the old days with Buddy saying how she used to sleep in his tee shirts and boxers. When Mavis asks about a chart on the wall depicting facial correlates to emotions, Beth explains that many of the children with whom she works learn emotions cognitively because the emotions do not come naturally to them. Mavis tellingly asks about being in "neutral," lacking any feeling. Beth replies that being in such affectless states is exactly how her charges often are. We wonder whether Mavis has returned to Mercury in order to get out of neutral and feel some emotion. During all this conversation, Beth is relaxed and welcoming. She is also attractive in the very effortless way in which Mavis describes the beauty of her books' teenage protagonist, but which hardly characterizes Mavis's own diligently constructed façade.

At the bar, Beth's band of mothers, aptly and humorously named "Nipple Confusion," plays with more gusto than talent. Mavis is non-plussed at the first song. Dedicated to Buddy from the stage by Beth, it is the favored tune that Mavis had been constantly replaying on her car stereo during the drive over from Minneapolis. Buddy smiles at Beth, who is obviously enjoying playing the drums ferociously and singing exuberantly "She wears denim wherever she goes." Mavis discomfits Buddy by reminding him how this song accompanied their sexual exploits, while dropping her head intimately against his arm. It is enough to make us in the audience cringe and the ever-present Matt to look on disapprovingly. After the performance, Beth is naively eager to take up Mavis's offer to drive Buddy home so she can hang out with her friends awhile longer. Saying goodnight, Mavis kisses an inebriated Buddy who, truth be told, does seem to reciprocate. Mavis soon joins Matt at a bar where he again tries to discourage her heavy drinking. As Mavis extends her visit to Mercury, Matt continues to play the Jiminy Cricket conscience to Mavis's wayward Pinocchio: warning and advising, questioning and admonishing. Unlike Pinocchio, however, Mavis ignores Matt's pointed directions, such as reminding her of Buddy's happy domesticity.

Woven through the film-story are voice-over scenes of Mavis writing the last installment of her young adult books. The series for which she is the ghostwriter is ending because its popularity has plummeted. The film intimates that Mavis's own glow is fading and that her values, encapsulated in the stories, are themselves aging poorly. The sad decline of her work is eventually and officially underscored at a book store where unsold copies are on a clearance table before being returned to the publisher. Here, Mavis's vanity is expressed in her insisting on inscribing a few of the books, since she is confident that her signature would be sure to increase their value. Mavis is miffed at the young clerk for pointing out that if she signs the books the publisher will not take back the remaindered copies, as these are unlikely to be sold (even though burnished with Mavis's inscription!).

The star of the books is Kendal Strickland, an obvious stand-in for Mavis herself. As in her own life, Mavis focuses on Kendal's beauty, noting that she was not just the prettiest girl in school, "she was a legend," even nominated for homecoming queen at a neighboring high school! A revealing trope in the film is Mavis filching portions of overheard teenage conversation to be recycled in her book. Discussing romance, for example, a girl in a fast-food restaurant calls unspoken communication between sweethearts "text chemistry," and Mavis immediately appropriates it. Mavis herself will use such a pilfered line on Buddy in the movie's extended climactic scene. The character of Kendal and the snatching of everyday teenage vernacular indicate the limits of Mavis's imagination, implying that although almost forty, Mavis is pretty much stuck in an adolescent mindset.

Mavis makes a spectacle of herself

At the name day celebration of Buddy's baby, Mavis fittingly faces humiliation. "Fittingly," because the announcement of the baby's entry into the world is what occasioned the launching of Mavis's reclamation project. Another manicure and a facial coupled with fastidiously applied make-up ready Mavis for the big day. The motif of the daily battery of beauty treatments resonates with the repeated entries into Mavis's final young adult novel. Both emphasize the importance of appearance to Mavis – in her protagonist as well as in her own person. In a side room at Buddy's home, Mavis makes her explicit overture to Buddy. He looks alarmed when she tells him that she is feeling everything that he is feeling. Mavis continues by saying that the last few days with him have been some of the best of her life. When Buddy seems surprised, Mavis reassures him, "You don't have to pretend." She then delivers a line she overheard a teenage girl intone to a friend (and that she has already incorporated into her last young adult story): "You're my moon, my stars; you're my whole galaxy!" Buddy pushes her away as she vainly tries to ensnare him in an embrace and kiss, blurting, "Mavis, what are you doing?" Yet Mavis persists, telling her old boyfriend not to be afraid, that they can work out a permanent relationship. Appalled, Buddy charitably tells Mavis, "You're better than this," but that she should leave.

From the top of the stairs, Mavis looks ruefully down on Buddy who is enthusiastically holding his newborn girl. She gulps down some alcohol and joins the group who have gathered outside where Buddy is going to give Beth a present. When Beth asks a disgruntled Mavis if she is alright, Mavis replies that she would be fine if she could get a real drink. Beth proceeds to bring over a pitcher of what looks like sangria and accidentally bumps Mavis, spilling the dark red concoction all over her new dress. As Beth hurries for something to help with the mess, Mavis bellows "Fuck you!" twice, and then calls the stunned wife a "Fucking bitch." The crowd is shocked into amazed silence. Mavis laughs and unconvincingly says, "It's a joke!"

Feeling the need to explain herself, Mavis bemoans the fact that this could have been her party because she herself had been pregnant with Buddy's child but miscarried when she was a twenty-year old. This revelation gives us a new angle on why news of Buddy's baby was the catalyst for Mavis's ill-conceived, abortive mission. It generates a flutter of sympathy for the unraveling woman who is making a spectacle of herself. Mavis pleads her case with Buddy's mother, reminding her how special and inseparable she and her son had been back in the day. Buddy's mother is quietly distraught and embarrassed for Mavis, as is her own mother. Earlier, when Matt complained of the lasting damage he suffered from the beating he had taken in high school, Mavis had chided him for living in the past. Unintentionally ironic, Mavis seems devoid of even a smidgen of self-awareness.

On cue, the garage door opens on Buddy pounding away on the new drum set for Beth, sporting the band's name. Befuddled by the crowd's lack of enthusiasm, Buddy wades into the subdued gathering of friends and family, and asks what's wrong. When Mavis asks Buddy why he invited her, she learns that he had not, in fact, wanted her to join the festivities, but that she was invited at the urging of his wife. Generous-hearted, and perhaps unperceptive, Beth held out hospitality to the cunning, jealous interloper. We wonder whether Mavis feels the contrast between the two women now in Buddy's life: the glamorous, conniving, envious ex-girlfriend thrown into sharp relief by the natural, unadorned comeliness of the wife whose wholesomeness is not merely on the surface. Buddy informs Mavis that Beth and others feel sorry for her, astutely observing that she is lonely and confused. Mavis asks Beth, "Do you hate me? Because I hate you!" Turning to leave, Mavis barks that she came back for Buddy and that she hates the town and its stench of fish shit.

Shame

Mavis shortly realizes that she has humiliated herself, as much by her foolish attempt to lure Buddy back into her life as by her vicious attack on his wife. Where else to turn, but Matt's lair, where he is working on his juvenile figurines. Confessing her disgraceful behavior, she proclaims, "I screwed up so bad." Whimpering, Mavis adds, "No one loves me. You don't love me." Matt trenchantly responds, "Guys like me are born loving women like you." Looking forlorn, Mavis tells him that she ruined her dress as a stand-in for recounting her actual, shameful behavior. As if the soiled dress emblematizes her blemished soul. After she and Matt partially disrobe, Mavis whispers "Hide me," when we expect her to say, "Hold me." The reason for this substitution is that Mavis is experiencing shame: feeling sullied by one's own actions and thereby revealed as morally deficient. Mavis has finally stepped back from herself, her scheme and the behavior it engendered, and viewed herself from without. She wants to hide, if only symbolically, in the arms of the only person who seems still to care for her, despite his partial knowledge of her perfidy.

Shame is an appropriate and healthy moral response to Mavis's hurtful and self-incriminating public display. We are encouraged by her admission to Matt. The truth of Buddy's life and her own callous, unrealistic plan (about which Matt tried repeatedly to warn her) seem to have penetrated her delusional, obfuscating interpretation of herself and events. Mavis at last seems to have learned to view herself through a moral lens, undistorted by the habitual pull of her vanity. One standard way of analyzing shame is to see it as the result of the individual feeling morally judged to be lacking in some important respect by an audience. On this view, the agent must see herself as identifying with the moral stance of the audience. This is certainly the case with Mavis. She views herself through the eyes of the community gathered at the name day celebration for Buddy's newborn girl. The exposure is literal and moral: the individual is literally exposed to others as morally flawed. The protagonist of the novel *Milkman* elaborates:

> In no way was it a weak feeling, for it seemed more potent than anger… often it was a public feeling, needing numbers to swell its effectiveness, regardless of whether you were the one doing the shaming, the one witnessing the shaming, or the one having the shame done unto you.
>
> (2018: 53)

As Gabriele Taylor argues, however, the individual need not be subject to an actual or even imagined audience: "He need not imagine an actual observer... All that seems necessary is that he shift his viewpoint... to that of the critical assessor" (1985: 58). Taylor explains that the actual or imagined observer may merely be the means by which the agent looks at himself and not itself ultimately responsible for the sense of shame. What is being observed and judged is not just the behavior, but the individual himself, "In feeling shame the actor thinks of himself as having become an object of detached observation, and at the core to feel shame is to feel distress at being seen at all" (1985: 60). Having identified with a critical perspective on himself, the person feels himself to be less than he had believed himself or wishes himself to be.

What is especially interesting here is the way vanity and shame both involve an audience or its facsimile. However, shame inverts the relationship between vanity and audience. Vanity seeks an audience to admire the object of personal pride: the individual's resplendent home, prestigious award, stunning mate. Mavis goes to great lengths to enhance her considerable physical glamor. She wants people to gaze upon her – men with longing, women with envy. And yet the audience gathered at Buddy's home is instrumental to her shame. Regardless of whether an actual audience is necessary to all cases of shame, such an audience is indeed operative in the case of Mavis's sense of moral dereliction. Exposure to her townspeople, appearing to them hurtful, lonely, and self-absorbed instead of beautiful and desirable, is then responsible for her asking Matt to "hide" her when "hold" would seem more likely. Circumstances have moved Mavis to see herself from an outside, morally disinterested perspective, impelling her to judge herself morally blameworthy. She needs to remove herself from exposure even when she is no longer literally visible to an audience. Finally, Mavis has arrived at the requisite self-consciousness. Together with the revelation about her youthful miscarriage, there is at last something about this preening, vain woman we can find to value if not like.

Shame is also aligned with humiliation in their common connection with exposure. Where we can be humbled without being exposed to the gaze of others, humiliation involves failing in some way, technical or moral, in front of other people. Being humbled and being humiliated are similar, in that both deflate our self-esteem due to an unwelcome experience. However, there are important differences between the two kinds of deflation besides the necessary public nature of humiliation. When humbled, we realize that we had overestimated our worth or ability and now adjust our self-assessment downward. But we are grateful for this correction in our self-knowledge, not angry. As Nancy Snow observes, "humbling experiences… are parts of the educative process of personal growth… We learn our limits through humbling experiences" (1995: 214).

However, when humiliated we are angry with ourselves for the failure; more subtly, we feel a measure of resentment toward those who have witnessed our coming up short. The individual's self-evaluation is forced downward by the censorious regard of other people and she chafes at their power over her. In Mavis's case, the failure is moral, hence also the shame. But we can feel that we have not measured up in technical tasks as well: not meeting the mark as an athlete, craftsman, or teacher, for example. We suspect that the ultimate failure for Mavis is not so much the moral failings born of vanity, her callous scheming or attack on Beth, but the technical one of not succeeding in reclaiming her lost love.

For consolation, Mavis sleeps with Matt having ascertained that he is still, after all these years, smitten with the former high school knockout and, though damaged, able to function sexually. During their coupling, we see shots of Matt's superhero action figures, as if in mute approval of his long-delayed, erotic triumph. In response to Matt asking her why Buddy was so important to her, Mavis replies that he is good and kind, and "He knew me when I was at my best," doubtless thinking of her youthful physical beauty. Matt disputes this by pointing out her vanity, noting that she looked more at her own reflection in the mirror in her locker than at him when he stood at his adjacent locker. Moral character as the standard of evaluation rather than appearance. Echoing an early scene with an anonymous date in Minneapolis, Mavis slips out from under Matt's arm and leaves his bed in the morning.[1] She dresses and goes to the kitchen and soon her moment of moral clarity dissipates under the worshipful gaze of Matt's sister.

During a conversation over coffee, Mavis asks Matt's sister, Sandra, if she knows Buddy's wife. Sandra replies that she does not like Beth. As if offering a reason for her animosity, the sister tells Mavis that she is prettier than Beth. But Mavis pushes on truthfully, saying that she has a lot of problems and that, "It's really difficult for me to be happy." After noting that other people like Beth seem so fulfilled when she is not, Mavis rightly admits, "I have to change Sandra." But instead of reflecting seriously about Mavis's plight, Sandra brushes off the accurate self-analysis and insists that Mavis does not need to change, pointing out that she is "the only person in Mercury who could write a book." Projecting her own adoration of Mavis, Sandra gushes, "Everyone wishes they could be like you."

Sandra also squelches Mavis's clear-eyed evaluation of the lives of the town's people. When Mavis wistfully muses how the people in Mercury seem so happy with so little, Sandra pooh-poohs their contentment as the result of their inconsequential, dead lives. This is unfortunate since Mavis had actually been on the mark about what a realistically happy life looks like in contrast with the superficial trappings of her own apparently more impressive circumstances. Sandra's concluding, resounding, "Fuck Mercury," elicits a "thank you" from Mavis. Her sense of Kendalesque superiority thereby restored, Mavis brightens and says, "I needed that [pep talk]." Although Sandra has helped Mavis regain her strain of vain superiority by lauding her looks and accomplishments, she is nevertheless rebuffed when she asks Mavis to bring her along to Minneapolis. Mavis curtly dismisses the plea, saying, "No. You're good here, Sandra," as if Matt's sister belongs in the place the younger woman has just derided as moribund.

We suspect that if it had been Matt chatting with Mavis over coffee instead of his sister, she would not have had such an easy path back into her former, haughty self-appraisal. Of course, we cannot know what the long-term upshot of such a different exchange might have been. What we do see is disconcerting and the film is uncompromising. It provides no bittersweet redemption for Mavis, but rather regression. A few sycophantic words wash over her, and Mavis is returned to her vainglorious perch. Why? The film suggests that the heavy, heady current of vanity, and the delusional perception of the world it imparts, is not easily diverted. This is who Mavis is: no less a young adult than her protagonist and readers, despite pushing forty.

In truth, the film-story may make Mavis too unlikable, possessing so few merely decent traits or impulses, let alone any genuinely sterling virtues. The one exception, of course, is her incipient self-awareness and the shame that it engenders, making it seem as though a redeeming reformation might be in the offing. But no, a few fawning phrases and Mavis is able to shake off the appropriate and medicinal moral gloom subsequent to her nasty display of misplaced injury. Why does the shame and accompanying reform, or resolve to reform, not persist? The film suggests that the moral sensibility evoked by her shame-induced self-examination recedes from view as Mavis ascends again into the cloudy heights to which vanity lifts her.

Note

1 This moment also resonates with an early shot of Jack, in *The Fabulous Baker Boys* (Chapter Three), exiting the bed of his one-night stand. These quick snapshots of Mavis and Jack capture the loneliness inherent in casual, transient sexual encounters.

Bibliography

Burns, Anna (2018). *Milkman*. Minneapolis, MN: Graywolf Press.
Garry, Ann (1982). "Narcissism and Vanity," *Social Theory and Practice*, 8, 145–53.
Kant, Immanuel (1963). *Lectures on Ethics*, Trans. Louis Infield. Indianapolis, IN: Hackett.
Nuyen, A.T. (1999). "Vanity," *The Southern Journal of Philosophy*, 37, 613–27.
Snow, Nancy (1995). "Humility," *Journal of Value Inquiry*, 29, 203–16.
Taylor, Gabriel (1985). *Pride, Shame, and Guilt: Emotions of Self-Assessment*. Oxford: Clarendon Press.
Tiberius, Valerie and John Walker (1998). "Arrogance," *American Philosophical Quarterly*, 35, 379–90.

Filmography

Kloves, Steve (1989). *The Fabulous Baker Boys*, U.S.
Reitman, Jason (2011). *Young Adult*, U.S.

Index

Note: Page numbers followed by "n" denote endnotes.

The Abduction of the Seraglio (Mozart) 73
Abrahams, Harold 9, 16, 86; college dash 9–10; experience of humiliation 17
admiration envy 67, 74
aesthetic virtues 3
Akeelah and the Bee (Atchsion) 101n1
Amadeus (Forman) 5–6; complex portrait 63–8; jealousy and musical transformation 71–3; loving the music, loathing the man 68–71; Salieri assists, creation and destruction 73–8
Andrew Neyman 34–41, 42n3, 42n4
Aristotle 11, 19, 23n7, 74, 92
arrogance 4–5, 8, 16, 22n5, 25–8, 32, 41, 82, 97, 104–6
arts 3, 24, 27, 37, 44, 49, 57, 76, 77, 84, 91, 93, 95
aspiration 91, 96; inform and motivate 84; non-moral aspect of 83
aspirational pursuit 98
Austen, Jane: *Pride and Prejudice* 25
authoritarianism 28–34

Baker boys 44, 47, 56, 60
Bernard of Clairvaux 15, 21, 23n10, 37, 70
Beth 107–8, 110, 113
betrayal 28–34
Billy Elliot 30, 84–5, 87, 90–5

Billy Elliot (Daldry) 6, 80, 85–6, 91–5
Bonnie 95, 97, 98
British Olympic 9, 12, 15
Brodie, Jean 4, 8, 33, 35, 41, 42, 42n2, 104; attitude exhibit 26; to change teaching methods 27; classroom charisma 24–5; high-handed characterizations 31; pedagogical arrogance 28; virtues of Franco 32
Bruce Pandolfini 95–100
Buddy Slade 102, 104–13
Bykovsky 88, 89

Camille Claudel (Nuytten) 86
"Cape Coalwood" 89
Casey, Sean 38, 39, 41–2
Cassio, Michael 70
Cavell, Stanley 48, 56, 62n7
challenges 9, 10, 21, 28, 42, 57, 80, 87
character 8–12, 16, 21, 25, 44, 49, 51, 58, 66, 70, 77, 78, 81, 98, 109; fictional 8; traits of 2
Chariots of Fire (Hudson) 2, 4; companion virtues 12–15; finishing race 21–2; forgetting ourselves 20–1; gratitude and god 18–20; humiliation, humility, and defeat 16–18; moral perspective of humility 10–12; two great runners 9–10
chess 6, 80, 81, 84–7, 95–100, 101n5

classroom charisma 24–5
college dash 9–10
companion virtues 12–15, 81
confrontation 55–8
Connolly 37, 38
consummation 54–5
courage 44, 46–8, 56, 61, 61n5

dance 6, 30, 80, 81, 84–5, 87, 92–5, 100
Darcy 25–6
defeat 16–18
desire 2, 5, 7, 22n3, 45, 57, 61, 66, 69, 72, 75, 76, 102
development 18, 83, 107
disposition 1–3, 7, 45
Don Giovanni (Mozart) 73, 76, 78

Ebert, Roger 61n6
egocentrism 27
Emersonian perfectionism 48, 61n4
Emerson, Ralph Waldo 46, 49, 56, 58, 61, 62n7
emotional vice 72
emotion-laced vice 71
emulative envy 64
envy 5, 8, 13, 14, 63, 70, 72, 74, 78n2, 104; admiration 67, 74; chronic and painful 66; complex portrait of 77; destructive 75; emulative 64; form of 65; primitive 64, 65, 77; sophisticated 65, 67; type of 64; vicious 77
essential growth 18, 57, 82, 96, 113
essential pursuit 8, 86
ethical theory 8
executive virtues 2, 3, 5; of perseverance 6
existential 8, 49, 56, 63, 67–8, 77, 80
expression, from within 91–5
external goods 57, 58

The Fabulous Baker Boys (Kloves) 5, 115n1; confrontation 55–8; consummation 54–5; fraternal fracas 58–61; new blood 52–4; trouble with Jack 50–1; virtue and talent 44–50
failure 6, 17, 25, 27, 35, 46, 47, 56, 58, 60, 75, 82, 113
feminine vanity 103

film: philosophy and 1–2; and virtue 7–8; *see also individual entries*
Fischer, Bobby 96, 98
Fletcher, Terence 4, 8, 33, 34, 40, 42, 101n3, 104; Andrew's relationship with 38; attitude exhibit 26; to change teaching methods 27; classroom charisma 24–5; pedagogical arrogance 28; pedagogical *modus operandi* 27; relentless attack 35; use of possessive language 36
Frank 44, 49, 50–5, 58–60
Fred Astaire 93, 95, 97–9
Fresh (Yakin) 101n5
fundamental dependence 12

Gaita, Raimond 44–7, 49
Garry, Ann 103
genuine virtue 9
Giotto 29
Good Will Hunting (Van Sant) 47
gratitude 13, 18–20, 23n8

habit 2, 8, 96
Hare, Stephen 14
Hayworth, Rita 61n6
Heidegger, Martin 28–9
Hill, Thomas 13, 20, 26
hobby 90
Homer Hickam 84, 85, 87–92
honesty 44, 47, 48, 51, 60, 61n4
Hudson, Hugh: *Chariots of Fire* 9 (*see also Chariots of Fire* (Hudson))
humble individual 18, 20
Hume, David 74
humiliated individual 17
humiliation 16–18, 22n5, 22n6, 59, 112; teaching as 34–7
humility 2, 4, 6, 16–18, 23n8, 61n1, 70, 82, 88, 98; lack of 13, 78; moral perspective of 10–12; paradigm of 11, 22n2; self-inflation in 26
humility-arrogance 69, 78

Iago 66, 70, 74
inspiration 84, 96; from without 87–91

integrity 5, 8, 44, 46, 61n1, 61n2; companion of 48; developing and exercising natural gifts to 61n4; lacking in 58; requires courage 47; second-order moral trait 45; understanding of 49
integrity-dereliction 48
intellectual virtues 3
internal/intrinsic goods 58, 62n9

Jack Baker 5, 8, 44–6, 49, 51, 55, 56, 58, 60, 61, 62n8, 115n1; complicated relationships 53; professional and personal relationships 54; trouble with 50–1
jealousy 71–3
Joan of Arc 32
Jo Jones 35, 39
Jonathan 97, 98
Joseph (Emperor) 69
Josh Waitzkin 85–7, 95–100, 101n4
justice 3–4

Kant, Immanuel 20, 46, 75, 83, 103, 104
Kekes, John 47, 57, 61n5, 86
Kendal Strickland 109, 114
Kissinger, Henry 26

Liddell, Eric 4, 9, 10, 17, 22, 22n2, 22n3, 23n9, 23n10, 82, 86, 94; belief in God 19, 20; Christian missionary 16; facets of 11; humbled individual 18; humility makes him grateful to God 13; moral gap between British officials and 15; religious compunctions 12; talent prompt generosity 14
Lindsay, Lord Andrew 13, 14, 18
Lloyd 50, 52–3
Lloyd, Teddy 27, 29, 31–3, 42n2
loathing 63, 68–71
Lowther, Gordon 30, 32, 33, 42n2
loyalty 2, 28–34

The Magic Flute (Mozart) 73, 75, 77
Marcel, Gabriel 29
The Marriage of Figaro (Mozart) 70, 72, 78

Mary McGregor 32, 34, 39, 41
Matt Freehauf 106–8, 110, 111, 113
Mavis Gary 6, 8, 102–5, 108, 113, 114, 115n1; makes spectacle of herself 109–10
Milkman (Burns) 111
Miss McKay 28, 32, 33
Miss Riley 88–91, 93
Mona Lisa Smile (Newell) 36–7
moral character 1, 4, 7, 8, 11, 69, 78, 98, 113
moral law 103
moral obligation 46
moral perspective 15, 17, 18, 21, 22, 22n4; of humility 10–12
moral principles 46–8, 61n4
moral psychology: ideas about 1–2; philosophical exploration of 1
moral superiority 69; belief in 67
moral trait 1, 7, 8, 12, 69; second-order 45
moral value 11, 14, 45, 83, 84
moral virtue 2, 3, 83, 100
motivation 5, 8, 31, 35, 45, 61n2, 85
movie experience 8
Mozart 1, 6, 13, 63, 67, 71, 75, 76, 86; *The Abduction of the Seraglio* 73; character and behavior 70; *Don Giovanni* 73, 76, 78; jealousy 71–3; killing of 68; lack of social grace 69; *The Magic Flute* 73, 75, 77; *The Marriage of Figaro* 70, 72, 78; Salieri feels toward 65; in Vienna 66
Mr. Bolden 89, 91
Mrs. Wilkerson 91–3
Murdoch, Iris: *The Sovereignty of Good* 42n1
music 6, 8, 37–8, 41, 44, 51–4, 60, 63, 67, 86, 91; loving of 68–71; transformation of 71–3
Mussolini 31–2

narrative affinity 7–8
New Year's Eve 54, 55
Nightingale, Florence 32
"Nipple Confusion" 108
non-moral value 45, 104
non-moral virtue 3
Nuyen, A.T. 102, 104

120   *Index*

October Sky (Johnston) 6, 80, 84–5, 87–91
openness 29–30
Othello (Shakespeare) 66

Palmer, Arnold 10, 11
Papathanassiou, Vangelis 22n1
Parker, Charlie 27, 35, 39, 40
passion 5, 19, 24, 28, 45, 46, 57, 59, 67, 80–8, 92, 100, 102
patience 6, 15, 81, 82, 98
perseverance 6, 81–83, 88–90, 92, 98–100
philosophy 41, 103; and film 1–2; pedagogical 28, 35
physical conflict, repetition and escalation of 59
pride 56, 58–9
Pride and Prejudice (Austen) 25
The Prime of Miss Jean Brodie (Neame) 4; arrogance 25–8; budding star 37–9; classroom charisma 24–5; loyalty, authoritarianism, and betrayal 28–34; second chance, second confrontation 39–42; teaching as humiliation 34–7
primitive envy 64, 65, 77
prostitution 57, 60
pursuit 6, 8, 80, 81, 83, 86, 87, 92, 93, 95; artistic 62n9; aspirational 98; essential 8, 86; of passion 92

quasi-moral virtue 83

Rawls, John 64, 66, 67
Reitman, Jason: *Young Adult* 102 (*see also Young Adult* (Reitman))
Requiem 75–8
resilience 6, 82–3, 89–90, 98
Richards, Norvin 10, 11, 19, 26
rocketry 6, 81, 84, 87–9, 100
romance 109
running 8–10, 12–14, 16–21, 23n9, 86

Sabbath 14, 15
Salieri, Antonio 1, 5, 13, 63, 67, 71, 86; assists, creation and destruction 73–8; confession 68; envy 70; facial expression 69; feels toward Mozart 65; jealousy 71–3; self-disclosure 64; self-esteem 66
Sandra Bartky 103, 113–14
science 80, 81, 84–5, 88
Searching for Bobby Fischer 6
Searching for Bobby Fischer (Zaillian) 80, 85, 95–100, 101n5
self-absorption 27, 41
self-assessment 11, 18, 25
self-awareness 21, 64
self-centered virtue 63
self-consciousness 92, 112
self-deception 9, 50, 56
self-discovery 80–7
self-esteem 66, 112
self-evaluation 17, 26
self-examination 25, 55, 114
self-exposure 17
self-indulgence 61n2
self-knowledge 11, 18, 51, 113
self-perfection 83
self-reflection 28, 94
self-regard 3, 5, 6, 9, 25; *see also* vice; virtue
self-worth 40, 105
sexual prostitutes 57
Shaffer Conservatory 34
Shakespeare, William: *Othello* 66
shame 111–14; salutary experience of 105
signature vice 104
Snow, Nancy 18, 70, 113
Socrates 28
sophisticated envy 65, 67
The Sovereignty of Good (Murdoch) 42n1
standard virtues 45
Stanzi 69, 71, 76, 77
substantive virtues 2, 3, 5, 45, 81
success 2, 4, 6, 11, 17, 21, 22, 24, 30, 41, 75, 80, 89, 98–100, 106
surliness 3
Susie Diamond 44, 47, 51–7, 60, 61, 62n8

talent: play, and parents 95–100; virtue and 44–50
Tanner 37

Taylor, Gabriele 44–7, 49, 64–5, 67, 75, 112
teaching, as humiliation 34–7
William M. Thackeray: *Vanity Fair* 102
theoretical structure 8
Tiberius, Valerie 25
To Sir with Love (Clavell) 30

unconventional teaching methods 28
uncooperativeness 3

vanity 6–7, 22n5, 108; and audience 112; force of 102–5; object of 103–5
Vanity Fair (William M. Thackeray) 102
vice 2–4, 6–8, 27, 66; in classroom 17; emotional 72; emotion-laced 71; of envy 13, 70; fabled unity of 104; philosophical perspective on 2; portrayals of 1; self-wounding of 63; signature 104; visions of 1; *see also* self-regard
vicious envy 77
da Vinci, Leonardo 29
Vinnie 95–7, 99, 100
virtue 2–4, 80–7; aesthetic 3; companion 12–15, 81; executive 2, 3, 5; film and 7–8; genuine 9; intellectual 3; moral 2, 3, 83, 100; non-moral 3; philosophical perspective on 2; portrayals of 1; quasi-moral 83; self-centered 63; standard 45; substantive 2, 3, 5, 45, 81; and talent 44–50; visions of 1; *see also* self-regard
virtue theory 1, 2

Walker, John 25
Watson, Katherine 36–7
Weber, Constanze 68
Weil, Simone 16
Whiplash (Chazelle) 4; arrogance 25–8; budding star 37–9; classroom charisma 24–5; loyalty, authoritarianism, and betrayal 28–34; second chance, second confrontation 39–42; teaching as humiliation 34–7
wholeness 46, 47
Williams, Bernard 45

Yakin, Boaz: *Fresh* 101n5
Young Adult (Reitman) 6–7; force of vanity 102–5; Mavis makes spectacle of herself 109–10; return of native 106–9; shame 111–14